IN PURSUIT OF
THE TWO LEGGED MULE

Malcolm G Nelson

Best wishes

Malcol~ G. Nelson

Published by Dolman Scott Ltd in 2016

Copyright 'Pursuit Of The Two Legged Mule' ©Malcolm Nelson 2016

Design and typesetting by Dolman Scott

ISBN: 978-1-911412-12-0

Dolman Scott Ltd
www.dolmanscott.co.uk

Dedication

This book is dedicated to my father, Walter George Nelson. Not only was he the man I respected more than any other, he was also responsible for my sense of values, and for me joining HM Customs and Excise, Waterguard in 1966. I cannot put into words how much I owe him.

About the Author

Malcolm Nelson was born on the 7th of August 1946 in Hackney, London, and was brought up in Loughton, Essex. He attended Kennylands Boarding School, Sonning Common, near Reading, and William Morris Technical High School, Walthamstow. He joined Her Majesty's Customs and Excise in 1966, and his career was unique in that he rose from the lowest rank, Assistant Preventive Officer, to very near the highest rank, Assistant Collector, without ever having to move away from the operational arm of the Department. In HM C&E promotion was invariably accompanied with, or obtained by a move to Headquarters or VAT. Somehow Malcolm was lucky enough to avoid this. During his career he worked on ships, on ferries, at docks, and airports. He worked in Russia, Malta and throughout much of the EU, but the vast majority of his career was spent at Heathrow. As a Senior Manager he was head of Passenger Services Division, Heathrow, when it became the first UK Customs Division to be accredited with the Cabinet Offices Charter Mark for service delivery.

He has been married to Carol for more than forty years and has three children; Mark, James, and Claire. He has one granddaughter, Neoma Mary, and a great grandson named Huxley. He now lives near Reading. He supports Spurs and Essex County Cricket Club, and drinks rum.

Since his retirement he has taken up public speaking and he now delivers in excess of one hundred talks a year, and lectures on board cruise ships. This is his second book. His first, "Forty Years Catching Smugglers" was published in December 2010.

Contents

Prologue

The mule, a passenger who it was suspected was carrying a commercial quantity of heroin, was being allowed to run. There were eight officers of HM Customs and Excise in the Concourse in Terminal Three. They were all dressed in "civvies," a disguise which involved taking off their uniform jackets and their black ties, and putting on their own everyday jackets or jumpers. The officers would follow the mule and see where he led them.

The passenger with the drugs was of little interest. He was just a courier, a mule paid to carry a package or a suitcase from A to B. He knew nothing of the organisation that had arranged the purchase and who would arrange the distribution. But whoever was meeting him; well they were important, they were a link to the distribution network, a link to the money men behind the importation. The mule was an illiterate Pakistani who spoke no English and had probably never been outside of his village in Pakistan before this trip. So there was every chance he would be met at the airport.

The officers worked in pairs and each pair had a radio, though the radios were very unreliable and mostly the officers relied on being able to see each other. The Officer who had intercepted the passenger in the Green Channel was one of the eight but he tried to keep his distance. He would act as the link with the Senior Officer (SO).

They were under strict instructions from their SO. 'On no account lose the mule.' Especially as he still had the drugs. Don't let him get into a taxi. There were no unmarked cars and no budget to pay for a taxi. If he gets on a bus follow him as far as you think it is safe. If he looks like he is going to the Underground, arrest him and bring him back. The Underground is dangerous and it is easy to lose a target, even one who doesn't seem to know what he's doing.

The passenger wanders about. Terminal Three is heaving. Up to eighteen thousand passengers pass through on a Saturday morning in the height of summer. The Pakair (the officers' colloquialism for Pakistan International

Airways) flight always attracts a whole crowd of people meeting those who are arriving. They have a tendency to congregate in large family groups, making it difficult for the officers to move about whilst observing the mule as he meanders aimlessly from place to place within the Concourse.

He approaches one of these family groups. The nearest Officer is too far away to hear what he's saying. He's probably speaking in Urdu and a couple of the officers do speak Urdu, but he's too far away for them to hear what he's saying. The Case Officer, that is the officer who made the original interception in the Green, makes a mental note to speak to this family when the time is right.

He wanders on, still nobody approaches him. He goes towards the exit where the taxis are lined up. The Officers get ready to grab him. But no, he realises he's leaving the building so turns round and walks back in. Obviously the person he expects to meet him should be inside the Terminal building. It's really chaotic inside the Terminal now, and the Officers are finding it harder and harder to keep "eyeball" on him. Some Officers have already taken up this type of jargon as it has filtered down from the Investigation Branch, but most of them find it hilarious.

Then, without knowing how, everybody loses sight of him. There's a couple of minutes of panic, before an Officer sees him coming out of the toilets. Two Officers immediately go into the toilets. Is there somebody there he could have made contact with? No, it's almost empty. A quick look in the cubicles just in case he's dumped his cargo. No sign of anything.

He then goes to the Information Desk. Now this is unusual. Does he know the name of the person he's supposed to be meeting? Is there going to be an announcement over the Tannoy. No there isn't. The girl behind the desk is looking bemused and she's shaking her head. He's obviously still speaking Urdu.

He carries on wandering around. Nobody approaches him. Eventually Frank - the SO who agreed the run - calls it off. It's forty five minutes since he was allowed to run. The mule might not be aware he's being followed, but there's a good chance his meeter has realised he was compromised. So Frank decides not to risk losing the man with the drugs.

The Case Officer arrests the mule and he is returned to the bosom of HM Customs in Terminal Three. A thorough examination shows that he has attempted to import 9.5 kilos of heroin, later the Government Chemists report will indicate a purity of 65%. It was concealed in the false top and bottom of a hard sided Samsonite suitcase.

Customs have triumphed in a minor skirmish in the war. One mule has been taken prisoner, but the victory hasn't been as complete as it would have been had the meeter been apprehended. For HM Customs this was just another minor incident in Pursuit of the Two Legged Mule.

Introduction

Her Majesty's Customs and Excise Officers (now part of Border Force) were a small group of men and women, much maligned and misunderstood by the general public. "In Pursuit of the Two Legged Mule" is the story of just how those few Customs Officers at Heathrow Airport waged their war on the drug smuggler. It describes their pursuit of that breed of men and women, the mules, who were prepared to risk everything, including their lives, to import prohibited drugs into the United Kingdom. It shows how those officers on the front line learnt as they went along with virtually no outside assistance. All of the incidents reported on within the book are real situations in which the author was either directly involved or had them related to him in person by the officers involved. The names of the offenders where they are given are their actual names. The names of the officers are in some instances their actual first names or nicknames, in others they are fictitious to protect those officers. The duties they performed were stressful, arduous, sometimes unpleasant, and at times dangerous. Although they were Civil Servants the image of the typical nine to five, tea dinking, grey suited Civil Servant couldn't be further from the truth. This book attempts to reflect the magnificent dedication they displayed as they carried out their duties.

**

The UK is now awash with drugs. Hard drugs such as cocaine and heroin, and the so called "soft" drugs such as cannabis and amphetamine. Various Government Departments (prior to 2005 this was HM Customs and Excise, then for a short period Her Majesty's Revenue and Customs, and now the Border Force) have battled against the flood of these drugs pouring across our borders. It is a thankless task which gets harder and harder as the drug cartels become more and more sophisticated in their methods of concealing these importations. It is also thankless because the officers involved know that the odds are heavily stacked in favour of the smuggler. Ninety thousand passengers arrive on average each day at Heathrow Airport alone. It is like trying to find the proverbial needle in a haystack. Especially as there are so few Customs officers based at Heathrow to cover all five Terminals, and the fact that successive Governments since

1971 have seen fit to reduce the number of officers available on a year by year basis. In 2011, SOCA (Serious and Organised Crime Agency) claimed that through the programme of upstream disruption they had embarked on we are winning the war on drugs, particularly in relation to heroin. This is somewhat supported by figures from the National Treatment Agency for Substance Misuse and from the charity 'Drugscope'. According to the 2015-16 Crime Survey for England and Wales fewer than 16,000 people said they had used heroin in the preceding month compared with 29,000 in 2009-10. However the author believes this means we have won some substantial battles but sadly, the war continues.

Although it always seems to have been with us, the battle against drugs is a relatively recent phenomena. It wasn't until 1916 that the Defence of the Realm Act criminalised the possession of, and trade in, cocaine and opium/heroin. During the First World War Harrods actually sold a "Welcome Kit" that contained Morphine and Cocaine. The idea of the Welcome Kit being to welcome our soldiers back from the front line. It wasn't until 1961 that the UN Single Convention on Narcotic Drugs listed cannabis as a proscribed drug. This was later incorporated into UK law in the Dangerous Drugs Act of 1964. The first record of widespread prohibition of any drug was when Napoleon banned his troops from using hashish when he and they were in Egypt in 1800. Obviously a man ahead of his time. In 1966 LSD was finally banned, although it did continue to be used as a therapeutic substance until 1971 when a total ban was introduced.

The first signs of commercial importations were seen in this country in the mid to late Sixties but this was mainly cannabis on ships through the ports, and on cars and lorries through Dover and Harwich. HM Customs were totally unaware of the impact that air travel would have upon the illegal drugs trade. This was especially true in respect to hard drugs such as cocaine and heroin where relatively small quantities are worth so much on the streets.

The Annual Report of HM Commissioners of Customs and Excise to Parliament shows just how this trade grew. In the late Sixties the Report only makes passing references to drug importations. By 1978 the Report shows that Customs Officers seized 6,600 kilos of cannabis, 27 kilos of cocaine, and 61 kilos of heroin. Then if we look at the figures for 1983 this figure has inched up to 62 kilos of cocaine and 219 kilos of heroin. Ten years later in 1993, the figures show 1,548 kilos of cocaine were seized and 1,506 kilos of heroin. This represented a 1000% increase. In the same year the figure for herbal cannabis was 11,000 kilos, and for resin it was 33,000 kilos.

If HM Customs needed reminding that dug importations were on the increase, they had the evidence right under their noses. Late in 1970 the Investigation Branch had information that a lorry with two containers was bringing in cannabis. They followed it from Dover, and despite losing it a couple of times (just how do you lose a massive articulated lorry?) they eventually apprehended the vehicle in the middle of London. The containers were found to have about a ton of cannabis in them. The offenders were arrested and duly found guilty at the Old Bailey. The trailer which had also been seized was parked outside the London Custom House on Custom House Quay right next to the pontoon that led to the Harpy. The Harpy being the floating Waterguard Station that sat in the middle of the River Thames, and which is now privately owned and is moored off of Butlers Wharf, on the other bank of the same stretch of river. After six months, surprise surprise, nobody came to claim the trailer, so it was decided to break it up. One lunch time, probably a Friday as that was paperwork day, three Assistant Preventive Officers (APO's), Messers Highstead, Kiy, and Nelson were on their way to a pub in Pudding Lane for lunch, when they noticed a couple of men with high powered drills about to start breaking it up. Being curious, and obviously not very thirsty or hungry, they stood and watched. It was amazing how easily the drill went into the frame and started churning out iron filings. It was even more amazing when the silver coloured filings turned a deep brown, and then because they were being subjected to a lot of heat, gave off the sickly sweet aroma of cannabis resin. The whole of the frame was full of resin. The APOs tried to lay claim to the seizure as it would have been a feather in their caps, and they were the only Customs Officers around at the time of the discovery. But they were told quite firmly by the Investigation boys to get lost. They, the Investigators, weren't looking for more glory, they just wanted to be able to brush it under the carpet to hide their embarrassment at having missed it in the first place. The Officers of HM Customs, through no fault of their own, really were a bunch of amateurs in those days. They simply had no previous experience to draw on. But they were learning, fast. It would be a while before they could keep pace with the opposition, but that day would come.

**

(2)

The Chase Begins.

Early days

An Officer, let's call him Geoff, was on duty in the Green Channel of the old Terminal One (now the Departures Building for Terminal Three), he was watching the passengers off of flight ME101 from Beirut pass through. Geoff at this point in his career was a Preventive Officer. He remained a Preventive Officer, but when the Department of HM Customs and Excise re-organised in 1971, and amalgamated with the rest of the Civil Service, he found he had lost his Preventive label and he was simply an Officer. He later gained promotion to Senior Officer (SO) or Higher Executive Officer (HEO) as it was sometimes known. It was early days, but later in his career Geoff would have a profound effect on the workings of HM Customs at Heathrow in pursuing the elusive drug mule. He, more than any other single person, would drag Customs kicking and screaming, into the murky world of the drug smuggler.

Geoff was in the Green Channel looking for drug smugglers. The Lebanon was a source country for a particularly potent type of cannabis resin known colloquially as Lebanese Gold. The label "Gold" came about partially because of its light brown colour, and partly because it was of such high quality it was worth its' weight in gold. The names given to the different types of cannabis were normally descriptive, Paki Black for instance as the name suggests was extremely dark, almost black, and it came from Pakistan. Both of these types of cannabis resin being particularly high in the THC that gives the drug its potency and it's psychoactive properties.

Geoff was looking for anyone that fitted the profile of a drug smuggler. He didn't use the word profile but that's what he was doing. Alongside him was his colleague, Dave S, who was also giving the ME101 his undivided attention. Their task was complicated because Lebanon was also a source country for illegal importations of almost anything. It was still known as Little Switzerland in those days and trade between the UK and the Lebanon was as varied as it was intensive. On one occasion a Lebanese national was stopped pushing a Geest truck through the Green Channel. Amongst the baggage were concealed 310 pornographic videos. The Officer, (nicknamed Alky) who found them, and a colleague, nicknamed Bats, had to look at all 310 just to make sure they really were pornographic. It was a dreadful task, and it took them ages. The videos were seized. The Lebanese gentleman appealed, so Alky and Bats had to look at them all over again. The experience left them in a desperate state!

Unfortunately for Geoff and Dave, the profile for a drug smuggler from the Lebanon was very similar to that of a business man smuggling other goods. They tended to travel alone; at this time they tended to be male; mostly they would look like business men; and the baggage would be sufficient to carry a reasonable weight. They could be any age from the late teens to the early sixties.

Dave stopped a man who fitted the description. He had already stopped at least a dozen people off of the flight with no success. This wasn't unusual, finding smugglers of any description is not an exact science, and it is never easy. An officer could go days, or even weeks, without getting a sniff of something illegal. The man he had stopped looked like a business man. He was carrying enough baggage to contain drugs or maybe commercial items. If he was a genuine business man, and he was carrying legitimate merchandise to sell or use as samples, then why wasn't he in the Red Channel. The passengers' reaction was typical of someone who had something to hide. Not necessarily drugs, but something. He was very calm. He was too calm. He said he was here on business but was very vague about the precise type of business. He hadn't gone into the Red because he was here to buy goods, not sell. So why did he have so much baggage. As Dave spoke to him he became less calm. His story was full of holes. He couldn't say where he was going to stay; who he was going to meet; how long he was staying; why he had paid cash for his ticket; how he was going to pay for the goods he claimed he was going to buy; he had no credit cards; and he had very little money.

Eventually Dave looked in the suitcase. Lo and behold there were several brown paper parcels inside it.

"What's in them?" asked Dave.

The only answer was a shrug.

Further examination revealed that the brown paper parcels contained approximately 20 kilos of the highly valued "Lebanese Gold".

Geoff, who had been showing a lot of interest while this was going on, asked the man if he was on his own.

Another shrug was the reply.

Geoff shot back into the Reclaim Hall. All the bags from the ME101 had been claimed and there was nobody hanging around the belt. Geoff raced back through the Green Channel out into the Concourse feverishly looking for someone who appeared to be just hanging about for no particular reason. The Concourse was reasonably empty; it was a quiet time of day. Geoff noticed a man, who, by the look of his complexion could well have come from the Middle East. Nowadays he might have gone unnoticed but the Terminals were much quieter in those days. A quick look at his passport identified him as a Mr Abbas who was resident in Beirut. At that stage Geoff had absolutely no evidence but nevertheless he arrested him on suspicion of attempting to evade the prohibition. He was led back into the Baggage Hall, protesting and protesting his innocence. It was amazing just how deaf Geoff could appear to be at times like this. He just didn't seem to hear him. He didn't bother to stop in the Green Channel and marched him straight into an interview room where he and his suitcases were searched. Mr Abbas, it transpired, had a similar weight of Lebanese Gold wrapped in brown paper parcels.

The interview revealed just how lucky Geoff had been. Mr Abbas had no details of where to go and who to contact. Therefore when his friend was stopped he had no choice but to wait for him. He'd come through first so he wasn't aware his friend had been stopped by Customs. Mr Abbas was essentially a sitting duck, or maybe a sitting mule.

This was the first known instance at Heathrow of multiple shipments of drugs. The two men were duly charged. They appeared at Uxbridge Magistrates Court, where Geoff and Dave laid the information before the Magistrates. There was no legal support available. Eventually they were committed for trial at Isleworth Crown Court. The jury of twelve good men and true (maybe there were one or two women) found them guilty and they were sentenced to three and a half years each.

**

Concealments became more and more devious as the enemy became aware that they were being targeted. Brown paper parcels were becoming scarcer, although they never completely disappeared. They carried on being much loved by the Jamaicans, the officers' theory being that they were just too laid back, to bother with a proper concealment. In reality it meant that they could claim they had been asked to deliver it and didn't know what was in it. Now the officers were finding that absolutely anything that could be hollowed out or sealed up with drugs inside was usable.

The imagination of the smuggler was inexhaustible. Brown paper parcels were one end of the scale but at the other end were clothing and carpets saturated with heroin solution. Because this was another advantage the smuggler had. He could change the format of the drug itself. Soak a carpet with heroin solution, allow it to dry, then when you reach your destination, soak it again and allow it to drain. Put the liquid on a low heat and boil away the water and hey presto you've got your heroin back.

If we start at the bottom then there's false soles and heels on shoes, or simply wrapped in socks, stockings or tights. Or if we go to other extreme then there's half a kilo or a kilo of cocaine underneath a sewn on wig. Possibly in between there's a specially made waistcoat designed not to show when wearing a shirt and jacket.

In the suitcase, as I've said, anything that can be hollowed out. Maybe coconuts or other fruit and veg such as plantains or yams. Cut them open very carefully so you won't see the join, scoop them out, and pack them with whatever drugs you choose. Then seal them up again and make sure the join is concealed in one way or another. Maybe as an added precaution let them rot a bit so they go black, they stink, and are covered with flies.

Cocaine could also be made into solution and put into bottles of "rum". The liquid then has a colouring agent added to it to make it a golden brown colour. Just the same colour as Caribbean rum. Then put it in bottles with the proper labels on, Cockspurs, Mount Gay, Appleton, all proper brands. After going to all this trouble find a compliant worker in a bottling factory, and there you have it. A sealed and intact bottle containing a liquid that looks just like it should look. How difficult will that be for the Customs Officer to detect? Extremely difficult! But if the smuggler wants to be even more devious then why not pay someone in a Duty Free Shop to put the bottles in a sealed Duty free Shop Box.

Another method was to put the drug somewhere where it won't look out of place. This is especially relevant when trying to smuggle cocaine. One of the many slang terms for cocaine is "snow". Why? Because it is very white in colour. So why not put it somewhere where there would normally be white powder. A tin of talcum powder perhaps, or maybe a carton of washing powder. Before the use of deodorants became widespread, many people used talc in the way we now use deodorants. So why wouldn't you have a tin of it in your suitcase? Also, many people coming from parts of the world where everyday products such as washing powder are not always readily available, will carry washing powder in their baggage. So nothing unusual to find a carton in a suitcase. Especially if it's still sealed, and doesn't appear to have been tampered with.

Another factor that helps the smuggler to conceal his or her wares is the fact that innocent people like to bring back home produce. So the Jamaican who lives here, returns to Kingston for a holiday, and quite naturally wants to bring back local produce to the UK. It reminds them of their spiritual home. Also it tastes better. So quite innocently, returning residents will bring back fruits, vegetables, plants, meat, tins of food, bottles of juice, and bottles of spirits. Anything that reminds them of home. So what could be more innocent than to have three or four tins of fruit? Especially when the labels are all intact. And even when you remove the label the tins have obviously been factory sealed. They haven't been welded back together in the garden shed. No, the Officer can see that the tin has been properly put together in a canning factory. The Officer is beginning to think maybe this person who fits the profile of a drug smuggler and has been showing all the classic signs of being up to something. Is actually one of the 99% of people who despite looking like a good bet, are actually totally free of guilt. So he takes the label off of another one of the tins; there are four altogether; this one looks good as well. So he shakes it, and he can hear the juice slushing about inside the tin. The problem the Officer has is that the wily smuggler might well have been cunning enough to put a separate container with a liquid inside the tin alongside the cocaine. Or as stated previously it might well be full of cocaine in solution. The cricketer Chris Lewis used the latter method of concealment when trying to smuggle 3.37 kilos of liquid cocaine in December 2008. A criminal act that has resulted in him being incarcerated at Her Majesty's Pleasure for thirteen years.

Double sided or more commonly the double top and bottomed suitcase. In the days when Geoff and Dave were dealing with the likes of Mr Abbas and his brown paper parcels full of cannabis, suitcases specifically manufactured to contain drugs had not been seen. But as the demand for hard drugs (and in particular heroin and cocaine) increased, the concealments became more sophisticated and the financial investment into them also grew. Double sided suitcases are not cheap and the profit margin on cannabis is not as great as it is on hard drugs, so while the main threat was from cannabis, the demand for this type of concealment was minimal. But as the numbers of cocaine and heroin addicts multiplied, so the frequency with which this concealment was used, also increased. The description 'double sided' covers a multitude of concealments, all of which involve the shell of the suitcase. Suitcases, such as a hard sided Samsonite, being used as one side of a double skin or shell. The second side being a false lining to the suitcase. With the drugs being concealed between the two skins.

Over the years these concealments (which included any adaptation of the suitcase shell to conceal drugs) became the most popular modus operandi for the smuggler until the swallowers appeared on the scene. But even then because each suitcase could conceal up to ten kilos whereas the average swallower only carried approximately half a kilo, they remained very popular. However although difficult to detect, they had one advantage to the Customs Officer. That was because of the extra weight, and very often the imbalance of the suitcase, they could be detected without the passenger knowing they had been rumbled. This gave the Officer the opportunity to 'run' the consignment without the passenger knowing. With most consignments that were large enough to be worth 'running' the Officer would have to reveal to the smuggler that he had been caught out. For example if you open a brown paper parcel and it's full of cannabis, well the person is going to know that you've seen it. He or she is going to know they've been caught. So it's no good saying:-

"That's alright sir. Off you go."

And then hoping he doesn't notice that the Officer and all his mates are following him outside into the Concourse. So the more sophisticated and professional concealments did have some advantages to the Customs Officer once they'd detected them.

**

Different Styles for Them and Us

It wasn't long before the 'wily smuggler' couldn't be trusted to simply hide drugs in his suitcase and if they were found put up his hands and say:-

"It's a fair cop guv, you've got me bang to rights."

15

The 'switch bag' and the 'rip off bag' routine would soon be upon us and these methods would only add to the problems for the Officers of HM Customs and Excise.

**

An Officer, let's call him Vic, was stood at the mouth of the Green Channel watching the TG, Thai Airways, from Bangkok. There had been a lot of 'Thai Sticks' coming in lately. Thai Sticks being a particularly potent form of cannabis which, as you might have guessed, came from Thailand and was rolled into the shape of sticks.

Anyway Vic was watching a man who looked like a Thai national who was flitting about like a cat on a hot tin roof. He was waiting for his bags but unlike everybody else he was flitting from one side of the baggage belt, to the other, and then back again. Then he went to the toilet. Then for some reason or other he took his ticket out. After that he stood still for a while. As the baggage started to appear he started moving around again. He took some rubbish, from his pocket, it looked like sweet wrappers, and deposited them in a bin. He went back to the belt. At last as an afterthought he went and got himself a trolley, and retrieved a large black soft sided suitcase from the belt. As he approached the Green Channel he appeared very calm. His previous behaviour had been replaced by a casual relaxed demeanour that contradicted everything that Vic had seen previously. Vic wondered if he'd just been worried about his suitcase. Lots of people, in fact most of us, worry that our baggage will get lost. And back then in the late Sixties a high proportion of checked in baggage did go missing. The most amazing thing about the Tel Aviv airport massacre in 1972 in which 26 people were killed by members of the Japanese Red Army was that the baggage that was carrying their weapons actually arrived. It was that bad.

Vic decided to pull him anyway. He fitted the profile, and he fitted the recent trend, of young Asian males, travelling alone, and looking very much like they were visiting these shores. Vic established that he was resident here, he claimed to be a student. The name on the Passport was unpronounceable and for reasons that will become obvious later Vic shortened it to Mr Stick. It was however a strange time for a student to be travelling. You usually had an enormous rush in September then a smaller rush in January and just a bit of a rush after Easter. This was the end of July. However Mr Stick had his reasons. He was coming to sort out his course as there had been problems last term. When asked how long he'd been at home, he said two weeks, but his Passport indicated it was only a couple of days.

Vic was becoming more and more unhappy with Mr Stick. It didn't help that he had a cash paid ticket, and the baggage tag was missing from it. His story was that he had gone home on business, but then he had to return because there was a problem with his next year's course. This of course, no pun intended, could have been entirely plausible. The business he had been back to Thailand to sort out was, as he put it, 'family financial affairs'. Very difficult to verify one way or another. He had documents to prove that he was indeed a student at Baliol College, Oxford; coincidently the same college that Howard Marks the infamous cannabis smuggler had attended. What he didn't have was anything that showed there were problems regarding next year's course. Later when asked if there was anyone who could be contacted to confirm what he was saying, he claimed there would be nobody there because it was the summer vacation. This of course posed the question:

"Just how was he going to sort it out if there was nobody there?"

Mr Stick agreed the suitcase was his, he agreed he had packed it and he said he wasn't carrying anything for anyone else. Vic asked Mr Stick to open the suitcase. He unlocked it and opened it.

The top layers were men's clothing. Mr Stick made no comment.

Underneath the clothing were four packages wrapped in black plastic.

"What have you got in these packages?" Asked Vic.

Mr Stick gave a very good impression of looking confused he lent forward and picked up one of the packages. Vic very quickly took it back.

"I don't know how they got there. No, hold on, they're not my clothes. I don't think this is my case."

Surprise, surprise. There then follows the rest of the pantomime. He looks for the Baggage Tags on the suitcase and on the ticket and realises that they're not there. This suitcase of course never had a Baggage Tag as it was never checked in, or if it did there was no corresponding tag to be put on a ticket.

"Very sorry Officer, make big mistake. Pick up wrong case. Look just like mine, very sorry"

Vic and Mr Stick return to the Baggage Belt in the Reclaim Hall, and sure enough there is an identical case to Mr Stick's. This case has a Baggage Tag but without any other labels. They return to the Green Channel and the suitcase is opened. Immediately Mr Stick recognises his clothing. Yes this is his case, he made a simple mistake. But officer you can see what an easy mistake it was the cases are identical. Anybody could have done it. Vic now has a whole lot of questions to ask him. Such as:-

"How comes you didn't recognise they weren't your clothes in the first suitcase?"

"Where is the tag from your ticket?"

This is later found in the bin that Mr Stick had been seen throwing some rubbish in. He's disposed of it because if he doesn't the scam becomes immediately apparent as soon as the Officer stops him.

He has then got to answer the question:

"Why did you pick up a suitcase that doesn't match your tag?"

Further examination of the 'dirty' bag revealed that the four packages contained a total of 20 kilos of cannabis in the form of Thai Sticks, hence the name Mr Stick. Vic had just involved himself in one of the first instances of a "switch bag" routine. The smuggler checks in one suitcase and an identical one is placed on the aircraft one way or another. When the smuggler arrives at his or her destination they pick up the bag with drugs in. If they are stopped and the drugs are discovered, of course it's not their bag. The famous, or maybe that should be infamous, cannabis smuggler, Howard Marks, used a version of this method when bringing drugs in via Geneva. There was Baggage Belt in Geneva that was used for international and internal flights. Marks, or Mr Nice as he became more widely known, would arrange for a fellow conspirator to arrive on an internal flight at the same time as he was arriving with a case full of hashish from Afghanistan. The cases, which were of course identical, would go round the belt together. Then the other man would pick up the bag belonging to Marks and walk through the Domestic Channel, where there were no Customs, and Marks would go through the International Channels with clean bag. If he was stopped, and he often was, of course there was nothing to find.

Now Vic made one mistake when he let Mr Stick get his hands on one of the packages. This made it more difficult to tie him down over finger print evidence. He kept saying, quite rightly, that he had handled some of the contents of the suitcase. But Vic could say quite specifically (and he was pushed and pushed about this by the Counsel for the Defence), that he had only touched the one package. And fortunately for Vic, Mr Stick's prints were everywhere. These were early days and later smugglers would be much more wary about handling the goods before packing the dirty suitcase, and Customs Officers would be much more diligent about making sure they didn't touch anything when they were searching the baggage. The simplest way of doing this was to make sure you opened the suitcase with lid between you and the passenger not sideways on as Vic had done. But as has been said before they were all on a steep learning curve in those days.

The good news is that twelve good men and true, or maybe, as I've said before, maybe ten men and a couple of women, listened to the evidence at Isleworth Crown Court. They decided that there were too many coincidences and unexplained mistakes and found Mr Stick guilty of attempting to evade the prohibition.

**

It was early days back then, and officers were having to learn fast. With no experience to draw on and no such thing as international co-operation in those days, officers literally had to learn on the hoof. The previously mentioned Geoff was at the forefront of most things that were going on. He linked up with two other Officers, another Dave and a third who we'll call Stuart, or Flash, as he was nicknamed. In the financial year 1971/72 they would seize more drugs than the rest of the entire Police and Customs in the UK combined. The three of them would have widely different career paths. Geoff would stay at Heathrow for the whole of his career. He would be a major influence in the war against the drug smuggler. He would also be responsible for training officers how to find drugs. He would also teach officers the incredible dictionary of drug slang. This was information that he gathered from every source possible. So that officers would know what to look for when reading through correspondence.

Geoff would make officers aware of the drug slang that was being used on the streets. It gave them an idea about what they were reading when they were looking through documents. An innocent looking phrase on a piece of paper could mean something quite different when translated from the drug slang. Officers soon became aware that if they were reading about horse or coke they were in fact reading about heroin and cocaine. These were obvious, but then they started to see the more obscure terminology. A simple note saying, "Make sure you've got plenty of Californian Cornflakes for when I get there". Might look like someone was thinking about their breakfast. But in reality they were making sure there was cocaine available wherever they were going.

One officer reading through correspondence noted that the traveller had a postcard that referred to meeting up with a young lady called Tina when he arrived in London. All apparently innocent, except that thanks to Geoff's training, the officer knew that Tina was also drug slang for crystal meth. Crystal meth being short for crystal methamphetamine a synthetic drug that gives a tremendous rush or high followed by up to sixteen hours of euphoria. Now this in itself wasn't of any use to the officer as the passenger obviously wasn't carrying anything. However it was information, and it would go on a Suspect Movement Report (SMR) with whatever other information the officer could glean from the passenger. This information would then go forward to the Intelligence arm of Customs to see if it fitted into any of the numerous jigsaws they were always working on. Was the person known, was the address known, were any of the people at that address known as dealers or suppliers?

On another occasion, an Officer, we'll call him Rob, proved that knowledge of slang could actually produce hard results. Rob had stopped a backpacker, who had just spent about three months travelling around the Himalayas. He was filthy, he stank, and his hair was rank. Rob had stopped him because backpackers were a good source of personal use jobs. Not commercial quantities, but they brought back small amounts of cannabis or heroin, and Rob had been having a lean time, his Senior Officer was on his back. He went through his haversack, took out all the filthy clothes. Looked through his toiletries, though there weren't too many of them. He had some of the usual junk, not drugs that people bring back from Nepal and places like that. There was nothing. Rob was rapidly losing interest. He wanted to carry out a search of person (SOP), but he didn't have any grounds. He was flicking through a bundle of correspondence that Mr Backpacker had in his rucksack to see if there was anything interesting. He wasn't really reading any of it, they were all from his girlfriend telling him how much she was missing him. Then he noticed a postcard showing a buxom blond on the front of it. That's a bit of a strange postcard for someone's girlfriend to send thought Rob. So he read it a little more closely. It all looked very innocent. A friend of Mr Backpacker's, not the girlfriend, was just keeping him up to date with the latest football and what was going on at home. However the last line was a request or maybe a reminder. "And don't forget you promised to bring me home a deck", it read. Very strange. Rob asked Mr Backpacker what this meant. Mr Backpacker said he didn't have a clue. But there was subtle change to his demeanour, he was now ever so slightly on edge, whereas previously, apart from the usual frustration at being stopped, he had appeared quite relaxed.

What Mr Backpacker didn't know, and he would have been even more worried if he had, was that Rob had just been on one of Geoff's Drug Familiarisation courses, and he knew that the word "deck" wasn't a reference to pack of playing cards or the floor on a ship, it was street slang for a packet of drugs.

Armed with this information Rob approached Pat the Senior Officer on duty. Pat, who hadn't been on the course, but who knew enough about Geoff's expertise, allowed the SOP to go ahead.

With an APO called Phil, Rob escorted Mr Backpacker into a Search Box and told him what was about to take place. Mr Backpacker promptly undid his trousers and retrieved a package from his underpants. The package contained eighty grams of heroin. Not a massive amount, not a commercial amount, although some of it would have been sold to friends and fellow students, but it would have been worth approximately four-thousand pounds on the streets.

**

Geoff would never lose his motivation. When he was promoted he would pace the Green Channel when high risk flights were going through, pointing out potential hits, muttering at officers to get their hands out of their pockets and do their jackets up. To Geoff, any officer who didn't look as smart as he possibly could was a "scruffy git". If officers worked hard, he was prepared to support them one hundred percent. But if they didn't he would make their lives hell. Even after he retired he was still returning to pass on his huge store of knowledge.

Dave moved uptown to join the Investigation Division and he would spend his career progressing the seizures that Geoff and others were making at Heathrow.

Stuart (Flash) would have a career that would take him on a completely different path. Having immigrated to Australia he joined their Customs service, and very successful he was too. However for whatever reason, maybe financial problems, or maybe because his new partner's family were heavily involved in drugs, Flash decided to swap sides and join the bad guys. There was strong suspicion that he was involved with importations of heroin into this country, but there was no proof. He suddenly changed his patterns of behaviour. When he came back here he would normally meet up with his old mates, including Geoff, but now this wasn't happening. Normally on his way through he would make a point of saying hello to the officers in the Green, but now he was just slipping through without a word. On one occasion he was stopped by an Officer called George. George wasn't happy with Flash but other officers told him "That's Flash McLean, he's one of us", so he let him go. He was filmed by the Police at his new partner's family home. It was all very strange. It was all explained later when he was caught smuggling heroin into Australia, concealed in dolls and footballs. Coincidently Flash's first seizure in Australia was heroin inside dolls and footballs. This was a prime example of poacher turned gamekeeper. Or should it be the other way around. Anyway for his crime he was found guilty and he was sentenced to twenty-six years in an Australian prison. What a very sad and sorry demise for someone who had started his career with so much promise.

**

In 1970 Geoff began going out the back of the Terminal so he could have a look at the bags before they reached the Baggage Reclaim area. Later Customs would focus on this work using "Tarmac Teams" In their early years these Tarmac teams would carry out all types of detection work on the Tarmac area. Indeed at one time they were more involved in seizing cars that had been imported but had had no import duties paid on them, than they were looking for drugs, cigarettes, tobacco, etc. But as they developed they would focus more and more on drugs, and in later years they would be phenomenally successful. They could identify which bags had drugs in simply by squeezing them, smelling them, feeling their weight. When there was information on individual suitcases they were able to find that suitcase amongst the thousands of suitcases that are moving around the Tarmac area at any time. In addition to these skills that had the experience to know when a suitcase was in the wrong place. If a bag wasn't where it should be, then why? Was it because it contained something that it would be better to keep away from Customs. Something that it would be better to take out through one of the many gates that were well away from any Customs Officers. These bags were called "rip off" bags, and the gangs that took them were called, and I'm sure you'll be amazed to learn this, "rip off gangs."

Anyway back to Geoff. He found that by going out the back he could look at more bags. He couldn't look in them but he could check out false tops and bottom or false sides. If a suitcase had false sides or more commonly a false top and bottom then the method was to stand it up as if to pick it up by the handle. Then squeeze the sides and take in a deep breathe through the nose. The case will be abnormally stiff, and will give off a faint odour of glue. Sometimes they would smell of mothballs put in the suitcase to confuse the dogs.

The first time Geoff did this he realised what a tremendous advantage it gave him. He was busy working away all by himself looking at the bags on the Pakair when he found two cases that he thought didn't feel right. They were very stiff and they were very unbalanced. They also appeared to be very heavy. He told the loaders to leave the cases there until he told them to put them on the belt. He then contacted his boss, we'll call him Phil. Although this was early days in the battle, in fact it wasn't really a battle it was more of a skirmish, some of the more aware members of HM Customs, including Geoff and Phil, knew that the mules were not important. It was whoever they were delivering to, the people meeting them, the meeters that they wanted. This would link them to the organisation and the money men. Anyway Phil, who would also end up, up-town in the Investigation Division, gave the go ahead for the run to take place. Geoff gave everybody time to get into position. He then told the loaders to put the dirty bags on the baggage belt. He nipped into the Reclaim Hall, watched an Asian looking gentleman pick up the bags, putting on his civvy jacket on the way through and removing his tie, Geoff followed him out onto the Concourse and into the multitude waiting outside.

I have stated earlier in this book that to a certain extent both sides were amateurs in the early days, and sure enough our mule, being closely followed by a group of whites males, dressed in identical blue trousers and white shirts, but with different jackets on, was immediately approached by another Asian looking gentleman. They shook hands, said hello, and proceeded towards the exit. The officers followed them to the car park and arrested them. Geoff had not only got two bags containing almost 20 kilos of heroin. More importantly he had his meeter. Later in the war, Customs would learn to let this type of run carry on until it reached its' final destination. But these were early days and they didn't have the resources or equipment to let it go off airport. Despite this, Geoff's success was a major step in the right direction.

After this Geoff made it his business to check out every high risk flight that came through on his watch, and gradually the practice was taken up by more and more Officers. Eventually 'Tarmac Teams' were formed specifically to deal with drugs and they then spent the vast majority of their time at the back of the Terminals working along with the dog teams.

**

The First Swallowers

It was 1973 and Chris was standing in the Green Channel of Terminal Three watching the passengers from the Syrian Arab flight, RG401 from Damascus, pass through. It was a high-risk flight not just because it was from the Middle East where drugs were freely available and very high quality cannabis was produced. On top of that it was the cheapest way of connecting from the Far East. As a consequence there were a whole lot of people who were travelling from places like Pakistan and India, who flew to Damascus and then connected to the RB401. Chris was working with another Officer who we might call Dave, although this was another Dave. Both Chris and Dave were heavily involved in drugs. Not in smuggling or using them, but involved in catching the people who were attempting to smuggle them.

Chris quickly pulled over a Mr White. He was travelling alone. He was scruffy and unkempt. He didn't look at ease. Chris pulled him and searched his baggage. He had a good story; he was resident in the UK he had been away to India and Nepal where he had been backpacking. He was extremely nervous but was trying not to show it. Experience tells Customs Officers that most innocent people are nervous and they show it. Or they act like they are guilty. The guilty person will try and act very calmly as if they haven't got a care in the world. This is just how Mr White behaved. But he wasn't doing it very well. There was nothing in the baggage, so Chris and Dave strip-searched Mr White. Still, there was nothing, but the Officers were becoming more and more convinced that they were onto something. They decided to take him into the box and have a word in private. This would often jog a person's memory and it gave them another chance to search his baggage in more detail. This was still early days for HM Customs as far as drugs were concerned, and the Officers were very aware that new concealments were being uncovered every day. Still there was nothing. Chris and Dave were quite new to the airport so they then consulted with two very experienced Officers. This was another Dave (they were everywhere in those days) and Bill. Dave was one of the true "seizure kings" of Heathrow and Bill would go on to specialise in training Officers for going to Court. This was his area of expertise and many Officers had cause to thank Bill for his advice on what to and what not to do when you were in the Witness Box in court. All four of them were of the opinion that Mr White was up to something.

At this point, out of the blue, the detainee asked to use the toilet. There was no reason to refuse him as there had been no cases of internal concealments in the UK at that point. He was allowed to go in private. Dave, the first Dave that is, checked the toilet after in case he had something concealed on his person that they had missed. He returned to the Interview Room. A little later he asked to go again. The Officers were now more than a little suspicious, but as he had pointed out the food in Nepal and India can do funny things to your stomach. This time they kept the door open but they stood back at a respectable distance. He went to the toilet. They could hear that he really was going to the toilet. He didn't do anything suspicious. Wiped his bum and flushed the toilet. Chris and Dave took him back to the Interview Room. Then the other Dave for some reason or other went into the toilet and looked down the pan, and what did he find? He found a lot of little brown packages floating around on the surface. Using plastic gloves he gingerly removed the packages and let Chris know what he had found. The Officers were all amazed; nobody had seen anything like this before. This was the first swallower. As with many of these things, they had stumbled across it because of their determination, their intuition, and their feeling that something just "wasn't quite right".

All in all Mr White only produced about twenty grams of "Paki Black", a particularly strong variety of cannabis resin, very high in THC (Tetrahydrocannabinol), but he was a swallower and he was the forerunner of hundreds and hundreds of swallowers. People who, in the years ahead, would bring tons and tons of drugs into the United Kingdom. Each swallower would bring in up 350 packages normally containing about half a kilo of either cocaine or heroin. Cannabis was only used in the early days when the swallowers were also amateurs and didn't realise the risk they were taking for such a small reward. At the peak of the swallower problem HM Customs at Heathrow and Gatwick would detain over seven hundred swallowers in one year.

**

It was now 1974 and Pete and Brian were in the Green Channel in Terminal Three. Customs were still only just beginning to understand the swallower problem at this point. *Had Mr White been a one-off?*

Three men were stopped off of the PK783 from Karachi. None of them had any good reason to travel. Pete and Brian were certain they were up to something. But what? Maybe they'd been away organising a run but weren't actually carrying this time. The bags were searched. Nothing was found. Their persons were searched. Again nothing was found. They were carrying some dental floss and some contraceptives. But so what. They'd been away for a few weeks and they were obviously going to have a good time so why wouldn't they have contraceptives? Considering where they had been it was probably a healthy thing to do. And why not have dental floss. Easier to carry than a toothbrush and toothpaste, and you don't have to rely on putting some dodgy looking water into your mouth.

The Investigation Division were around and they took an interest in what was going on and decided that two of the men were worthy of further investigation, so they carted them off to their HQ in New Fetter Lane. The third man, a Mr Wimberley, they decided wasn't up to anything. Brian and Pete weren't satisfied and they pleaded with Geoff - who was now a Senior Officer - to let them keep him overnight. They weren't particularly thinking he was a swallower, as there had only been Mr White so far, but they knew something wasn't right. Fortunately for them this was prior to the Police and Criminal Evidence Act (PACE) so the grounds for detention didn't have to be as specific as they do since that Act came into being. Geoff happily gave his permission and they settled down in one of the Interview Rooms. They brought in some bedding and a mattress and settled Wimberley down for the night. They locked him in and took it in turns to sit outside the door.

Later on, HM Customs would fully realise just what a dangerous situation swallowers were in, with all those packages of drugs inside them, and they would never be allowed to be on their own and out of sight. They also didn't realise the lengths that swallowers would go to retain their drugs, and that they would pass and re-swallow the packages if necessary. As soon as Customs were aware of these dangers the practice changed and officers would sit and watch the swallowers through an open door. If they were in trouble because the drugs were seeping through the packages into their bodies, the officers would have a greater chance of realising this and could call in the paramedics. Even this wasn't always enough and in one year there were three deaths in Custody caused by packages bursting inside swallowers and causing a massive overdose. On top of the three fatalities there were at least a dozen near misses that were averted by the prompt action of the watching officers. The other reason for watching through an open door (not through a window or on CCTV) is that if the swallower was trying to pass and re-swallow the packages then the officers would certainly notice. Even if an undue amount of activity under the blanket didn't give it away, then the smell certainly would.

Back to Mr Wimberley. Geoff returned to work the next day really early. He was worried about Wimberley. When he got there everything was quiet. Pete and Brian were outside the door and everything had been quiet overnight. However there was the most horrible smell all the way down the corridor. Pete and Brian probably hadn't noticed because it had crept up during the night. When they opened the door the stench almost knocked them over. Wimberley had passed several packages during the night and he had tried to hide them along with the faeces that had come out with them. There was muck everywhere. All in all Wimberley had thirty packages of cannabis. Thirty bundles that were simply condoms tied up with dental floss. In the early days this was the preferred method. Now Customs realised the swallower problem was here to stay.

In these very early days the methods of retrieval were bizarre to say the least. The offender hovered above a waste paper bin and dumped into a plastic bag. Then either the dump was poured into a sink and water poured on with the plug partially open to let the faeces wash away but retaining the packages in the sink. The packages were then flicked from the sink into another clean plastic bag using a metal coat hanger. Or, if there wasn't too much waste matter, the bag would be rolled up to bring the packages to the top and again they would be flicked from that bag into a clean bag using a metal coat hanger. Whichever method was used it would not have met with the criteria as laid down by the Health and Safety Executive, but it would have made an excellent game at a village fete; certainly much more entertaining than fishing ducks out of the river or throwing balls at coconuts. In both instances the ability of the officer with the coat hanger was of paramount importance. If he was no good then there would be packages and faeces flying about all over the place. Also the catcher needed to have excellent eye arm co-ordination.

By the time Gary, a young Texan, had been apprehended with another batch of 30 packages of cannabis inside him, Customs had become much more sophisticated. By then the officers were using a Portaloo, and emptying the faeces and packages into a colander. Then they washed the faeces away down the sink with a spray attached to a tap. For some reason or other they were always cream coloured plastic colanders. Not red or green plastic or even metal. No, they were always cream plastic. There were probably very good reasons for this but whatever they were they left the author with a hang up about cream coloured plastic colanders. He still can't have one in his house to this day. Using the Portaloo was better than the coat hanger method but it still wouldn't have met the criteria laid down by the H&S Executive.

I mention Gary because he was unusual in the amount of time he was detained. Gary had arrived on a "Red Eye" flight from New York. An Officer, let's call him George, not the same George as we saw with Flash McLean, was watching the flight with a particular interest in returning business men who looked a good bet for having exceeded their other goods allowances. Businessmen liked to buy suits in New York, they were cheaper than the UK, and they were of much better quality. However, they attracted a whopping 34% duty and tax, and as the allowance was only ten pounds, there would be a fair amount to pay. These were still the days of seizure rewards so George was very interested in the businessmen. As he was running his eyes over the passengers, Gary appeared. Now Gary stood out like a sore thumb. He was obviously not a businessman. He was dressed in jeans, trainers, and a leather jacket, and he was carrying a shoulder bag and a guitar. He sported a short beard and a ponytail. He looked like a hippy. In fact he looked more like a hippy then most hippies. What was he doing on the Red Eye? For one thing it's dearer to fly on one of the Red Eye flights. The airlines aren't daft, they know most of the seats are being paid for by large companies, so up go the prices. Back to Gary. What was he coming here for? He didn't look like he was a UK resident. He looked more like he was coming from Woodstock. The one in New York State where they have the big music festival not the one near Oxford.

George stopped him. He established he was a Texan coming to the UK on a short holiday. He had a three-month visitors stamp in his passport. He was intending to stay at the YMCA near Piccadilly in London. He had very little money, but he said he was going to get some bar work to tide him over while he was here. He had a return ticket. It all seemed ok. However George wasn't happy. There was nothing in the baggage, there was nothing on his person. Still, George wasn't happy. There was something about the way he was answering his questions and something about his body language that wasn't right. He had started very relaxed. Too relaxed, in fact. He then started to get a bit fidgety and nervous, began to throw questions back at George, and became a bit lippy.

George: "Is this your first trip to this country?"

Gary: "Naa I'se beeh hyarr dozens o times."

George: "Dozens of times, really!"

Gary: "Yeah dozens and dozens of times".

Then he wanted to know what would happen next.

Gary: "So what happens after you stopped searching ma bag? Yo gonna frisk me? Cause you won't find diddley squat"

Roughly translated in Texan 'diddley squat' means nothing, or nothing of any importance.

This was typical of the secondary body language/behaviour that an officer would expect from an amateur mule. He suddenly realises that his little bluff acting relaxed hasn't worked and he doesn't know what is going to happen to him if the drugs are found. He hasn't thought it through that far but now he's furiously wondering where it will all end. So he becomes slightly confrontational, a little bit aggressive.

What George did find was a little pack of dental floss. Not necessarily incriminating but at the time, the favourite type of swallowers package was the condom tied up with dental floss mentioned previously. It was doubly strange because Gary hadn't packed a toothbrush or toothpaste. Maybe he was going to get them here. Still it was strange, George felt that someone who cared enough about his teeth to pack dental floss would have remembered his toothbrush and toothpaste.

George decided to question him further in an interview room. He didn't actually arrest him. In reality he didn't have grounds to arrest him, but as this was before PACE he decided to detain him just to question him further. In George's experience things often became much clearer when people were isolated and a little bit disorientated.

The first thing George did when he was in the interview room was to explain that he had brought him here because he was worried about his health. Gary was confused. So was Georges jockey. His jockey being the officer who would assist him and witness the interview and the investigation. George explained that he had a feeling Gary had swallowed some drugs. There were no EMIT (Enzyme Multiplied Immunoassay

Technique) machines to test urine at this time but although there was no agreement with Hillingdon Hospital to carry out x-rays, they could generally be arranged. However they weren't used as automatically as they were later on in the pursuit of the two-legged mule. So George couldn't prove it. But he knew Gary was worried about something, and he had very little money with him. So little in fact George was surprised that HM Immigration had allowed him in.

He was offered food, and it was explained to him that he was going nowhere until he had had at least one good-sized dump. He didn't want anything to eat and he couldn't go to the toilet. If you can't go well you can't go. Ken the Senior Officer was also convinced that Gary was up to something. PACE wouldn't come along until 1984, so it was all up to the SO. Ken said keep him as long as it takes. When he said that he had no idea that it would take seven days. By this time Officers knew that the normal time period to extract a stomach full of packages was three or four days at the most. But no, Gary held on for seven long days. Nothing had happened after the normal amount of time had elapsed, so it was decided to seek permission to x-ray. It was a convoluted procedure at the best of times but Gary made it worse by demanding his human rights and threatening to sue if he was put in mortal danger by being x-rayed. What George received for his trouble was some of the clearest x-rays ever seen. He could actually count the thirty packages.

Holding out for seven days wasn't the record. That was held by a heroin addict by the name of de Groot who lasted a whole twenty one days, and after all that he had nothing. He just couldn't provide the proof. De Groot did provide the officers with a great deal of entertainment. He was allowed to call his mum in Amsterdam on several occasions. And the officers could hear him telling her:

"But mumma I want to go, but I can't go, and the officers won't let me go until I do go."

This was in response to her admonishing him for not complying with our requests that he provide the necessary proof that he wasn't carrying any heroin internally.

There were obviously two types of "go" being discussed by De Groot and his 'mumma'.

Things were easier with Gary as after 48 hours of George working on him and convincing him that he was in mortal danger Gary started to eat and eat and eat. He also admitted, after the x-ray, that he had thirty packages of cannabis inside him. Despite all the eating he didn't have a dump until six of the seven days had passed. I wonder why that was the case, the reader may well be asking themselves at this point.

After he had been charged Gary told George the whole story.

"Georgie boy", he said. They weren't just on first names by now they had gotten into nicknames.

"It was like this. We is just about to land. We can see the runway. I'm all belted up in ma seat, when I can feel them packages a welling up inside o me. I undid the belt and made a dash for the can (toilet). As soon as I get in there one o them there stewards is a banging on the door tellin' me to get back to ma seat and belt up. I didn't know what to do, so I just stuck the stopper (sink plug) in the hole. I threw up the packages. All thirty of them and...... Well I just fished them out and swallowed them again."

This pretty story was not appreciated by George and his jockey as they were on the point of going for lunch. However it did show the lengths desperate people would go to. And it did explain the seven-day delay. Firstly they had calculated that the packages had been swallowed about 24 hours before the aircraft landed. And secondly, his digestive system had obviously been severely traumatised by the invasion of thirty condoms full of cannabis and had thus closed down for a short period.

Gary was an amateur (a very lucky amateur). He had risked his life for thirty packages of cannabis. Madness!

**

The early years were full of errors and officers were constantly learning as things changed. They had to be reactive, as there was no information or experience to enable them to anticipate the next move the opposition would make. This was especially so with swallowers. As stated previously, at first officers would actually shut the suspect in an Interview Room. These rooms had no windows so they could be getting up to anything. Some of these rooms actually had washbasins in them and some of them had air conditioning ducts. There were radiators, they had desks and chairs in them, and wastebaskets. In fact they were perfect for a swallower to hide his or her packages, or to pass them and re-swallow them. The idea for doing this being that eventually the officers would believe they didn't have anything. Even when we had x-rays of the packages they would still do this in the hope that we would believe we'd got them all. To help convince us of this some would swallow the vast majority of their load in one go, let's say two-hundred and eighty out of three-hundred. There would then be a delay of perhaps three or four hours when they would swallow the rest. When questioned and shown the x-ray evidence they would admit to two-hundred and eighty. They would hope that when they reached two-hundred and eighty Customs would relax their guard and they would then be able to pass the packages later when they'd been taken before the Magistrates and removed to prison. This would enable them to use them as currency when they reached their final destination, and maybe get a slightly lower sentence when they went to Court. It took a while for officers to realise that people were doing this. When they did they realised that the only way to be sure they weren't simply "going through the motions", again please excuse the pun, was to watch them face to face twenty four hours a day, and to make sure they had two substantial clear dumps.

When Terminal Four was built, HM Customs insisted on cells with small observation windows being included within the accommodation. But even this wasn't good enough with the swallowers, because the door needed to be open. As has been mentioned before this was mainly for health and safety reasons, when a prisoner is in distress you are more likely to notice if you have direct sight through an open door, but also because if the prisoner was trying to pass and re-swallow the packages the smell would give them away. Even though by this time the prisoners were put into white Zoot Suits, and the stains would make it obvious what was going on, they still tried. Some prisoners were so badly dressed that they got quite upset when they were finally leaving us and they had to put their own clothes back on. They really like their Zoot suits.

What also didn't help in Terminal Four was that the one-way glass specially requested by HM Customs for prisoner observation purposes, was installed the wrong way round. Prisoners who weren't swallowers would have the door shut and the officers would just open the flap and check on them from time to time. The first prisoner in Terminal Four to have his door shut on him was a Mr Lakhani, a Gujarati gentleman from Ahmedabad in Gujrat State in Pakistan. Imagine the surprise on the officers' face when he opened the flap to make sure his prisoner was OK and all he could see was a reflection of his own face staring back at him. Once the doors were shut the prisoners could see us but we couldn't see them! Nice one BAA.

**

3

Looking and Learning
(1975-1992)

It was the time of their lives. Somehow it wasn't real. For a lot of officers it was like a huge game. But of course it wasn't a game. It was a war- but it was a phoney war. The smugglers would try one method and Customs would catch on. So the smugglers would try something else. And sooner or later Customs would catch on. It was serious, but it was serious in the fun way as Mr Nice - otherwise known as Howard Marks, would have us believe. The massive increase in consumption of heroin and cocaine that was to occur from 1979 onwards, hadn't happened. As soon as the bad guys shifted exclusively into Class A the whole thing became a war of attrition. Men like Leroy Winston Montereaux, of whom you will read more later, appeared on the radar and officers had to up their game once more.

There was however an element of Customs pitting their wits against the smugglers. It was almost as if there was this real life game of chess going on. But a game of chess in which nobody would ever be able to say, "Checkmate".

Tarmac and the Rip Off bags

The Tarmac was a generic term that described all the work that occurred at the back of the Terminals on that great swathe of concrete where the aircraft sit dis-gorging and refilling themselves with passengers, suitcases, fuel, and catering. The areas at the back of the Terminals were populated by Tarmac Crews, these were two Officer Crews who as time went on spent most of their time looking at suitcases before they, the suitcases, were put on the reclaim belts and disappeared into the Terminals. This was the moment the dogs would also get a chance to have a good sniff to see if there were any indications. Along with the Tarmac Crews there were Rummage Crews; these normally consisted of one Officer and two or three Assistant Officers. These crews would search aircraft and deal with any high-risk aircraft crews. The other crews would be cleared through "Crew Clearance" where they went through a mini Terminal but had to produce a written declaration on a form-C142. The Tarmac and Rummage crews would also spend a lot of time in the Transit Sheds. Looking for strange routes. Why is this suitcase coming from Islamabad going to Stockholm via Heathrow? Why isn't it going direct? Is it a rip-off bag?

As time went on and the smugglers became more and more devious in the routes they would use, the Tarmac crews became invaluable. A good Tarmac Officer would be able to trace a suspect bag no matter what circuitous route it was proceeding along. To the layman, the Tarmac Area with all the vehicles charging around all over the place would appear chaotic, and so to a certain extent, it was. However there was always method in the apparent madness, and a good Tarmac Officer would always know when the lines of that method were being blurred. This could mean the wrong bag in the wrong place, for instance, or the wrong person in the area, the wrong vehicle on the wrong route. The Tarmac Officer would know if an Aer Lingus loader was somewhere he shouldn't be. "What's he doing there?" Would be the next question. What's that Air Canada lorry doing on the stands normally used by Pan Am or TWA. They were an invaluable source of information and they were worth their weight in gold.

Customs officers were looking for drugs in bags coming through the Green Channel, and sometimes through the Red Channel. For instance a Singaporean businessman arrived once every two months from Singapore. He went into the Red Channel and declared an extra bottle of Johnny Walker Red Label. Not the more expensive Black label, no it was the Red Label that wasn't available in the UK for a number of years. The Officers in the Red duly charged the passenger on his extra bottle of spirits and let him go. Then unluckily for the passenger on this particular trip the Officer in the Red had only just finished his training. He didn't really know what he was doing. He didn't know about profiles and trends. He just didn't think the businessman looked right. In one respect he was wrong, he really was a genuine businessman who had legitimate reasons for travelling here. But the Officer decided to look in his brief case anyway. What did he find? Well he found five kilos of 'smack'. It was estimated the passenger had made at least twenty trips. If he had brought in five kilos each time then he had amassed a total of one-hundred and fifty kilos.

Anyway, back to where we were. Customs officers were looking for drugs in bags coming through the Terminals and through the Channels. Red or Green. So the wily smuggler decided it might be a good idea if the dodgy bag or suitcase didn't actually go through the Terminal. And so the "rip of" bag was born.

How did it or how does it work? Well the organisation the other end (the people wanting to get their drugs over to the UK) will arrange for the bag or suitcase with the drugs in to be placed on board an aircraft bound for these islands. Now they might do this in a variety of ways. They might actually check it in using a fictitious passenger and a bent check-in clerk. Or they might use a real passenger, but this is risky because if Customs find the bag before the passenger leaves the airport they might be able to trace the bag to the passenger before he disappears. Also he might be stopped and in those days the ticket would show the number of pieces of baggage. Or they might rip the bag on to the aircraft. This way the bag is brought through one of the many gates that abound on the perimeters of most airports and then taken to the aircraft side or taken to the back of the check-in, by a member of the gang. The bag is then placed with the other genuine bags. On arrival at the UK airport a rip off gang will be waiting. They will know how to recognise the bag and they will rip it off from the belly of the aircraft where the baggage is stowed, or when it is on its way to the back of the Terminal and goes into the Reclaim Hall. This gang will be genuine gang of loaders and they will spirit the bag away through one of the many gates out of the airport. They will then deliver the bag to wherever they have been instructed to deliver it. This will probably be a car park or some such public place without too many prying eyes.

The advantages for the smuggling organisation are immense. They don't have to come into contact with Customs; the rip-off gang are taking all the risks; and they know nothing except what the bag looks like and where to take it. Nobody from their organisation takes any risks. The only thing that could go wrong is that a Customs Tarmac Team decides to go to the aircraft and watch the bags before they leave the belly of the aircraft. But even then they have numerous chances between the aircraft and the back of the Terminal. Suitcases and bags are always falling off of the dollies; that's the little open sided carts that transport the bags to the Terminals. So it's easy to career round a corner lose a couple of bags and as you stop to pick them up stow the dirty bag somewhere where it can be picked up later. Or the rip-on gang will have made sure the case has a baggage tag showing that it is in transit to another airport. It will then go to the Transit Shed to be re-directed. It can then be picked up at the Transit Shed as and when the rip-off gang decide. At the gate the risk is non-existent. The BAA Security guards aren't interested and if HM Customs are in attendance then they just drive past and go to another gate. News of Customs doing Gate Checks would go round the airport like wildfire. It's all too easy.

**

It was in the early eighties and an Officer, Keith a typical 'scouser' with rapier like wit, was working at the back of Terminal Three doing the bags on the BA262 from Kingston, Jamaica. He was in a good mood. His beloved Liverpool had just become champions again and it was his Scheme Rest Day tomorrow. To his way of thinking it couldn't get much better, but actually it was just about to. The 262 was high risk for cannabis and cocaine. It was one of the most productive flights and consequently there were Tarmac Officers everywhere. Keith had just finished looking at one bag he wasn't happy with, but he decided to let it go. He was puffing a bit; he wasn't as fit as he used to be. The loaders were just opening a fresh container full of bags. As Keith looked up a suitcase fell out of the container landed on the floor with a thump, and disgorged loads of packages wrapped up with tape. Keith thought it was manna from heaven and promptly claimed the seizure as his. It would turn out later that the suitcase contained twenty-five kilos of cannabis.

The bag had a tag on it showing that it was the property of a Mr Glasgow and was going on to Melbourne. Or was it the property of a Mr Melbourne going on to Glasgow. It doesn't really matter which way round it was because when Keith and his 'oppo' (for arguments sake we'll call him Bob) checked it out the name was fictitious. The bag had clearly been ripped on in Kingston by airline personnel or people connected with them. Security had been avoided and a false tag had been put on the suitcase.

The Britain to Australia connection became well known over the next few months. There was a bag for a Mr Manchester transiting to Adelaide, a Mr Birmingham on his way to Perth. Even a Mr Stoke on Trent on his way to "Wagga Wagga!" The operation was obviously being managed by someone whose geographical knowledge was limited to the UK and Australia. If the perpetrators had ever been brought to justice, and they never were, a simple geography test would have been very useful in establishing their guilt or innocence.

This was all good work by the Tarmac Officers but it showed up the advantage of rip off bags to the smuggler. After several months of picking up rip off bags with twenty-five kilos of cannabis in each one, there were no names in the frame. When the seizures dried up Keith and Bob did wonder if it was just because the perpetrators had run out of towns and cities in Australia and Britain to link them to. Or perhaps they were just fed up with losing their cannabis and they switched countries.

**

It was 1991 and Keith, not the previous Keith, another Keith, was in the OITs office. OITs stood for Operational Intelligence Teams. He was very interested in the Bogota flight. Bogota was very high risk for cocaine. The major drug cartels such as the Medellin and Cali cartels had flooded the USA with coke and now they had turned their eyes to Western Europe and in particular to the UK.

The OITs spent an awful lot of their time looking at passenger lists. Looking for little tell-tale signs that would indicate that the passenger might be of interest to us. Apart from names of known suspects they would be looking for anything unusual. They would be especially interested in people who seemed to be taking strange routes to get back to the UK. Just why would a passenger go direct to Bogota or Lagos or Bangkok but return via Brussels? It could be something quite innocent. If the traveller was a businessman then he could well have business in Brussels, although maybe not so much in the future. But on the other hand it could be something much darker. It could be because they think we will almost certainly be looking at the Bangkok, the Lagos, and the Bogota, but they think we don't often look at the Brussels. They're right on both counts. So this sort of strange routing was of great interest to the OITs.

Perhaps the most notorious case of using devious routes to put Customs off the scent was seen in the case of two young girls, Karyn Smith and Patricia Cahill. In July 1990 these two little innocents had been spotted by an OITs Officer working in Terminal Four. Pete - the Pete we met previously with Mr Wimberley the swallower - had some good contacts with the airline check-in girls (purely professional of course). One of them gave him some information regarding two young girls who had come to the check-in on the evening of Sunday the 6th of July, to buy tickets for Bangkok on a KLM flight. What raised the KLM girls' suspicions was that the tickets were being bought by, as she described him, a chap with a "dusky" complexion wearing a dark shirt and white suit, does sound a bit like the Man from Del Monte, and most importantly he was paying cash. Nothing wrong with the dusky complexion, a lot of Pete's friends and colleagues had the same complexion. But paying cash for two expensive airline tickets was unusual. Maybe someone was trying to blur the audit trail? It transpired that Cahill and Smith had met him in a nightclub in Birmingham and he offered to pay for a holiday to Bangkok. Just like that, aren't some people generous? But strangely they didn't know his name. The KLM check-in girl knew from conversations she had had with Pete that cash transactions were a prime indication that drugs were involved, and even if it wasn't drugs the they were up to something. Just ask yourself, who pays thousands of pounds for anything, in cash? Unless of course they are up to something and they don't want an audit trail to lead back to them. This need for cash was and is, although not so much so as in the past, the Achilles heel of the drug organisations. That is, if they have such a thing as an Achilles Heel.

Pete observed Cahill and Smith on the Monday when they boarded the plane for Bangkok via Amsterdam. He then set wheels in motion and the girls were followed from the moment they arrived in Bangkok. They did none of the usual holiday things. They didn't visit temples, go to clubs, or spend time in the famous night markets. They stayed in their hotel most of the time. Then they made a couple of trips up country, but came back empty handed. Eventually, the Thai authorities stopped them as they were about to leave Thailand. They had approximately thirty-two kilos of heroin worth four million pounds on the streets of the UK, concealed in tins of sweets. But were they coming straight back to the UK, or maybe coming back via Amsterdam, the same way as they had gone out. No they were coming via Amsterdam and the Gambia. Had this not been picked up on the way out? Would Customs have been waiting for them? Probably not.

What happened to Cahill and Smith? They pleaded their innocence claiming the drugs had been planted on them. They thought they were carrying tins of sweets. The press in the UK proclaimed their innocence even claiming that they were a diversion, or a decoy, as the Independent suggested. If they were a diversion it was a really expensive diversion or decoy, four million pounds worth of heroin is a lot to lose. The Thais weren't having any of it and eventually the two young ladies ended up in Bang Kwang Prison, otherwise known as the Bangkok Hilton, but not to be confused with the hotel of that name. Cahill, who was probably the more guilty of the two, received a sentence of eighteen years, and Smith the elder by one year, was put away for twenty-five years.

Then in 1993 along came the cavalry in the shape of the Prime Minister, Mr John Major. The tabloid press, in fact most of the press, mounted a campaign to have the girls released. They were having to endure dreadful conditions and it just wasn't fair. So Mr Major petitioned the Thai authorities, and a Royal pardon was granted. These girls were undoubtedly dupes, but there can be little doubt that they knew they were doing something illegal. Nobody pays for you to fly to Thailand, sit in a hotel for a week then fly you all the way back again just to drop off some sweets in the Gambia on your way back.

However, back to Keith. He was having a good look at the BA 258 from Bogota. The passenger list showed two ladies from Northern Ireland, holding Irish Republic passports. Their journey was terminating at Heathrow but their two bags were booked onward to Brussels. Of course the two ladies could have had separate tickets from Heathrow to Brussels but this was unlikely. The whole situation simply screamed "rip-off". The ladies would get off at Heathrow and disappear. The two bags would be taken to the Transit Shed and from there they would be ripped off.

Keith passed this information on to the SO on duty on the Tarmac that evening. This SO was called Chris and he was a fiercely competitive Westo who liked nothing better than turning over the bad guys, especially if it was one of his teams that did the turning over. This gave Chris a bit of a problem as he had a very keen and experienced Officer by the name of Ken on that evening in charge of the Rummage Crew. Now Ken shouldn't actually have been there but he had swapped shifts with another Officer by the name of Ian. The most logical thing to do would have been to get Ken and his crew to do the transit bags in the Transit Shed, where the Brussels bags would be going, and to use his Tarmac Teams to do the London bags. But this would have meant someone that is Ken, who wasn't on his team, getting all the glory. So Chris, with his competitive side coming to the fore, switched them round and directed Ken to do London bags and his own team to cover the transits. This way his team would pick up the bags for Brussels and get the drugs and the brownie points, and it would go towards his end of year targets. It shouldn't be like this but that's what you get once targets and Performance Related Pay enter the arena. To be fair in reality most times it doesn't get in the way;

it actually creates a healthy climate of competition. Sometimes, however, it did create problems.

Ken realised that he had got the short end of the stick, but he was still thinking on his feet. He contacted Chris to see if Hold Five was being covered. Hold Five was where all the loose baggage, as opposed to the baggage in containers, was held. It was an ideal place for a rip off because if Customs weren't around the baggage was readily accessible. Some of these loose bags would be transit bags. It turned out that Hold Five wasn't being covered; Chris didn't have enough bodies. Ken, who was never slow in coming forward, suggested that his "linked" Rummage crew (that is the crew linked to his on the roster), led by a badminton playing Officer by the name of Alan, could cover it. Chris agreed and deployed Alan's crew accordingly.

Ken told his crew to get a move on and they went through the London bags like a knife goes through butter. Then, being the helpful Scouser he was, he made tracks for the Transit Shed to give the Tarmac lads a hand. They pulled up in the car and as Ken jumped out and started to walk past the containers he noticed a bag sticking out of one of them with a Brussels tag on it. Sure enough it had one of the names they were looking for. He was in the process of opening the case when over the radio he heard the Alan's Rummage Crew informing Chris that they had located the second bag in Hold Five, and it was positive. Ken examined his and saw that was positive as well.

Twenty five kilos of cocaine in each bag. Chris didn't know whether to laugh or cry. Fifty kilos of coke was brilliant, but sadly for him none of his crews were involved. So no brownie points for him.

As Ken and Alan wheeled their suitcases into Terminal Four they were surprised to find that not only were Keith and the rest of the OITs there, the Investigation Division had also turned up. The Division were pretty smart by this time but this was a quick response even for them. It transpired that they were there looking for the same two ladies. Two Columbian employees of BA had noticed the two ladies at check-in in Bogota airport. In particular they had noticed that two Columbian heavies accompanied the girls. They passed the names and the information on to the Drugs Liaison Officer (DLO) who at the time was an ex Heathrow Officer who we'll call Des. He set the wheels in motion and the ID in London was informed. They set their own wheels in motion but their wheels weren't as quick as the OITs and the Rummage Crews.

The two ladies were apprehended. The ID boys and girls went off to raid an address that they had obtained from the ladies. When they got there nobody answered the door, so they invited themselves inside and found it was ready for a party. There was banner declaring that it was "a drug free zone. Ha! Ha!" There was nobody in the flat but they must have left in a hurry because on the table there were two neat little bundles of cash with £5,000 in each. The two women were sentenced at Isleworth Crown Court to fourteen years each; this was the maximum at the time. IRA involvement was suspected but never proved.

This rip off had failed but Customs knew that very often it succeeded. Otherwise they wouldn't have continued to try to use it.

**

Roger or ROTA (Roger of the Airport) as he was known, was working at the back of Terminal Three. It was 6.45, it was a Friday morning and ROTA had just returned from a short holiday on the Isle of Wight. He was working with Keith the 'Scouser', who we have already met. Keith wasn't his usual chipper self, his usual running mate, Bob, was away on leave or at Court, or playing rugby. Anyway whatever the reason was he wasn't there and Keith wasn't his normal self. The Tarmac teams worked so closely together that when they were split they were never really happy. Despite this they were as usual working their socks off, looking at the bags from the PK flight from Rawalpindi. This was a high-risk flight, it was hard work, and neither of them was particularly happy. They were systematically pulling cases off, pushing the sides, or the top and bottom depending how you look at them. Sniffing them to see if they smelled of glue or maybe mothballs to confuse the dogs. There were no dog teams around that morning. The mood however changed dramatically when ROTA pulled off a small hard sided Samsonite briefcase. The Samsonite was incredibly heavy for such a small bag. He tried to press in the sides to see if there was any flexibility. There was one side but the other was rock solid. The whole attitude of the pair of Officers changed completely. Keith could see that ROTA was on to something, and the hairs on the back of Roger's neck were standing up. Pulling out his massive bunch of keys he found the right one and opened the case. Inside were a few personal items and the most obvious double bottom he had ever seen. He closed the case again and tried to stand it upright, but it was so heavy on one side that it kept falling over. If it hadn't been so serious it would have been laughable. ROTA and Keith knew that they had a sizeable amount of what was probably H, it could possibly be Paki Black, but that was unlikely in this sort of concealment.

Keith nipped into the Terminal to organise the observation of the suitcase and the courier when it came through. The local Investigation team were alerted, the run was organised. It was the meeters and greeters that Customs really wanted. The mule would know nothing about the organisation behind the attempted illegal importation but the meeter, well he might well know a lot, and if they could follow him who could say where it might lead. This run was going to be particularly difficult as it was a Friday morning in the middle of the summer and as usual the Concourse was heaving. There were more than three thousand people milling around waiting for relatives and friends. It was going to be tricky.

The SO in charge of the Investigation team, we'll call him Ron, and his sidekick, we'll call him Welly, had a really difficult decision to make. They were going to run it, that wasn't the question, but how many Officers to put out there? Since the death of Peter Bennett, an Investigating Officer who was shot dead by Lenny "Teddy Bear" Watkins, safety was on everybody's mind. He needed to make sure that there were plenty of Officers so that if it came to a confrontation Customs could physically overwhelm the bad guys. But if he was to put out too many would it cause confusion; the radios weren't that reliable, and couldn't always be used in a public area for fear of giving the game away. It was a long time before discreet radios attached to lapels would be available. On top of that, if there were too many people wandering about apparently doing nothing, would it spook the bad guys, would they realise something was going on and abandon the courier to his fate?

Once everything was ready and Ron had all his people in place the case was put on the belt. Ron was co-ordinating in the Reclaim Hall and Welly was in charge in the Concourse. From the front of the Green Channel Roger watched it going round and round on the belt. Then an Asian looking man picked up the bag and put it on his trolley. He didn't look any different to the hundreds of other Pakistanis that travel on the PK. He didn't look nervous; he was travelling on his own, which was a good sign as 99% of drug smugglers travel alone. It makes sense why risk two people going down for one cargo? Also the story the courier is going to tell if stopped will certainly contain more fiction than fact, and it's harder for two people to get their lies right than it is for one. So the man pushing his briefcase on a trolley walked into the Green "Nothing to Declare" Channel. He proceeded half way down the Channel, nobody intercepted him; everybody knew that this was Roger's job. Roger called the man over and asked to see his passport. He established that his name was Mohammed Khan, he was a resident of Pakistan, and he was coming here to visit relatives. Nothing dodgy about that, thousands and thousands of Pakistani nationals visit these shores every year to visit relatives. Mr Khan seemed to be very relaxed. Was he too relaxed, Roger wondered? Was this someone who had been telling himself, "If I'm stopped I'm not going to act guilty or nervous? I'm going to act relaxed and at ease, just as if I've got nothing to hide." Roger checked the ticket. The tag on the ticket matched the tag on the briefcase. This confirmed it was Mohammed Khan's briefcase.

Roger: "Is this your bag?"

Looking very pointedly at the ticket and the tag.

Khan: "Yes this is my bag."

This was important, it meant he couldn't use the switch bag routine, or deny ownership when questioned or at a later date when he appeared in Crown Court. The ticket also gave Roger one other important piece of information. It was cash paid. Always a good sign. Drug smugglers invariably had their tickets paid in cash. In fact everything to do with drug smuggling is paid in cash. Not only is there no honour among thieves, there's little trust among them either. But on top of that, importantly with cash there is no audit trail. So Roger was extremely pleased to see that Mr Khan had a cash paid ticket.

Roger didn't hold him up for long; he didn't open the case. He didn't want Khan to become suspicious or his welcoming committee to get the jitters. It was, to use the jargon of the time, a light tug. He let him go, and Khan (still very relaxed) left the Green and proceeded to the Concourse and merged into the hundreds of people waiting outside.

Khan obviously knew where he was going. He wasn't expecting to be met at the airport; he headed straight for the Underground. Ron had Officers covering all the exits. He was prepared to follow Khan anywhere but on to the Underground. If he'd taken a bus they would have followed. If he'd taken a taxi or he'd been picked up in another car then an unmarked car would have followed. Even if he'd decided to take another flight, as long as it wasn't to another country, they would probably have followed. But the Underground was considered too dangerous, other people get in the way, it was too easy to lose the person, too easy to swap bags. Just not worth the risk. Ron gave the word for Khan to be arrested and brought back to the Customs Hall, where Roger and Keith were waiting for him.

The case was examined, and a white powder, that gave a positive reaction to the opiate field test, was found in the false bottom of the case.

Khan was first interviewed by Roger and Keith and then by the Investigation Division boys from up town. Unusually Khan agreed to call a telephone number that he had been given to use on arrival or in case of an emergency. This was definitely an emergency, though probably not the kind of emergency Khan's minders had in mind. He called the number with an Official Interpreter listening in. The conversation was short and sweet. "This is Khan", said Khan. The person on the other end didn't identify himself. He simply blurted out an address in Southall, said, "Go there and wait for further instructions", and then he banged the telephone down.

With such a charming invitation the ID felt they couldn't refuse. Roger as the Case Officer accompanied them to a normal residential house in Southall. The people in the house were promptly arrested and removed. They of course knew nothing about any drugs and had never heard of anyone called Khan. This in itself must have been a record bearing in mind they were of Pakistani origin and there are millions of people who have the surname Khan originating from that part of the Sub Continent.

They then sat at the address for two whole days waiting for something to happen. But nothing did. The telephone number proved untraceable and disconnected when it was tried again. So by the third day they decided to call it a day. The bad guys had probably been watching the house and had seen HM Customs arrive, and decided it was time to make themselves scarce. Roger got to go home for the first time for three days.

This was a very typical job for the Tarmac Teams. What wasn't so typical was the ease with which Khan complied with the request to use the telephone number. There was obviously no code as Khan said so little. But perhaps he was expected to say something else and when he didn't his contact gave him a false address totally unconnected with the organisation. What also wasn't typical was when Roger and Keith took the 2 kilos of white powder to the Government Chemist in Waterloo. The chemist confirmed that there were 2015 grams of heroin; nothing surprising there. Brownish white powder coming from Pakistan, it would have been more surprising if it hadn't been heroin. No what was amazing was the purity. Roger and Keith couldn't believe their eyes when they saw the purity was 100%. This was incredible because at that time the normal purity was about 40%. The chemist re-tested it and it still came out at

100%. Not wishing to bring an element of doubt to the Court proceedings but it is almost certain the Defending Counsel would have tried to cast doubt on the accuracy of the test; the chemist decided to state that it was only 95% pure with a street value of two million pounds.

Khan pleaded guilty at Reading Crown Court and received a sentence of six and a half years at Her Majesty's Pleasure.

**

Now, if what happened to ROTA in the previous incident was a typical day at the office (not that any offence was a typical day at the office), they all needed an amazing amount of hard work and dedication. What happened when he was working with Dave, another colleague, was definitely not typical.

Dave, or Rocky as he was more commonly known, and Roger, were a Tarmac Team, radio call sign Tango 8. They were carrying out a routine patrol of the Tarmac Area. They weren't doing anything particular, there was no specific information; they were just patrolling looking around seeing if anything cropped up. They weren't needed at the back of the Terminals checking bags. The PK787 from Karachi was down so they made their way round to where it was parked and decided to have a look on board.

The aircraft was like an ants nest with people rushing everywhere. The caterers were on de-catering and re-catering. The cleaners were on cleaning the passengers' area and the toilets; both these groups were deemed very high risk. The engineers were buzzing around, making sure aircraft was fit for purpose. The aircraft was being re-fuelled, the loaders, also high risk, were in the belly unloading the baggage. Roger and Rocky needed eyes everywhere. They had decided to search the interior of the aircraft, a surface rummage, to make sure nothing had been stashed with the intention of having it picked up by one of the many many workers who were quite legitimately getting on and off the aircraft. The cleaners especially, and caterers were high risk because they were poorly paid compared with most airport workers and their security clearance was also at a lower level. There had also recently been a seizure of ten kilos of heroin from a cleaner in Terminal Three. The drugs had been dropped off by an arriving passenger who was carrying it in his hand baggage. The cleaner concealed it in his cleaning trolley, and would have simply wheeled it out through a Control Point, had HM Customs not apprehended him.

As they ran up the steps "Hari", the PIA Station Manager, greeted them. He looked very relieved to see them. He nodded towards a passenger who was still sitting in his seat. He was in the front row of the cabin just inside the door. He looked like he was drunk which was a bit unusual but not exceptional. Except that this was a PIA flight and Pakistan is Moslem country. Consequently there is no alcohol on board and the cabin crew confirmed that he didn't bring any duty free spirits on board with him.

Rocky spoke to him and asked to see his passport and ticket. The passenger eventually complied. It didn't happen straight away because the passenger seemed to be having trouble understanding Rocky, and the Officers were having trouble deciphering the slurred responses. It was all a bit bizarre as he was Canadian and they should have been speaking the same language. The passport showed he was a Canadian national who should have disembarked in Amsterdam and caught a KLM flight for Toronto. Just how he had managed to stay on board was a mystery, but of course security was much slacker pre 9/11 and as long as the numbers were right nobody really worried whether or not they were actually the right people. There was probably some poor passenger back in Amsterdam who had been refused permission to board because they had the right number of people. The man's passport also told Rocky that the man had only stayed in Pakistan for eight days. Canada to Pakistan is a long way to go for just eight days. He claimed he had been on business, but he was very unclear about what his business was. This made it even stranger. If it wasn't business, what was it? Why would a Canadian visit

Pakistan if it wasn't business? Not to visit family, and surely not for an eight day holiday. There could only be one reason. It was business, but not the legal kind. There is a very good market for drugs in Canada. The usual route for drugs to Canada would be up through the USA, and over the land boundary. However Pakistan is a source country for both heroin and cannabis, so why add the risk of getting the drugs in and out of the USA? Why not try the direct route? Rocky was becoming more and more convinced that he was dealing with a swallower and that there was a very strong reason to believe that the packages inside the Canadian were seeping. Being aware that the man was in great danger and that if one of the packages actually burst it would be fatal, they carefully helped him down the steps to their waiting car. Then they got him as quickly as they could to the Heathrow Medical Centre. The doctor examined him and passed him" fit to be detained but not questioned." This put Rocky and Roger in a bit of predicament, as they didn't actually have any grounds to hold him. Appearing drunk on a Pakair flight isn't actually an offence. However the doctor agreed that although he wasn't fit to be questioned he was fit to be x-rayed. Much to their relief the x-ray showed that he had a number of small packages floating around his digestive system. They now had grounds to arrest him, so they did. But as they were still very worried about him, and it was thought that the packages might seep further, or even burst as they were being passed, it was decided to take him to Hillingdon Hospital.

The two Officers of Tango 8 stayed with the Canadian in the hospital and during the next twenty-four hours he produced thirty-three condoms tied up with dental floss and containing approximately 2 kilos of cannabis oil. These were big packages. This man was full of surprises in every way. Cannabis or hash oil is a very unusual and very potent, it is the purest form of the drug. It's so potent that although it is a form of cannabis it is actually classified Class A, whereas herbal cannabis or resin are Class B or C depending on the whim of the Home Affairs Committee or the Prime Minister at the time. It is in the same bracket as heroin, cocaine, or crack. One of these thirty-three packages was obviously leaking and this is why he appeared drunk. He was in fact as high as a kite, he couldn't speak properly, he couldn't understand what he was hearing and he was very close to overdosing.

Well the two R's were now feeling quite pleased with themselves. A man's death had been averted and they had themselves a nice little job and a very rare one at that. The only problem they had now was, what to do with him? He hadn't actually broken any laws in this country, as he wasn't intending to bring the drugs here. He wasn't intentionally intending to evade the prohibition on importation into this country. In fact he was trying to evade the prohibition into Canada, but because of the state he was in he had turned up here by mistake. So he couldn't be charged with anything here. When he was told about the situation and that when he was well enough he would be free to go he just couldn't believe his luck. He was off the hook. But as it turned out he wasn't off it for long. The drugs were seized and he remained in hospital under guard. This was because technically he had never arrived here and he definitely wasn't going to get permission to stay. Quite understandably Her Majesty's Immigration aren't that keen on overdosing swallowers. Once the hospital discharged him he was escorted by Tango 8 to the Air Canada aircraft that would repatriate him. This was where his luck ran out. Sat next to him, all nice and cosy, was a senior member of the Royal Canadian Mounted Police. To you and me that's a "Mountie"

This fine gentleman, minus his horse, had been attending a conference in London with UK Law Enforcement Agencies. He had become aware of the case and asked if he could help to bring the passenger to justice back home in Canada. At the time there was minimum sentence of seven years for conspiring to import drugs such as cannabis. Several condoms full of hash oil were given to the Mountie to take back as evidence. When they arrived back in Toronto the passenger was arrested and charged with conspiracy to import. Three other arrests were made, other quantities of drugs were found, and the "drunk" received a sentence of ten years when he finally ended up in court.

The two R's had hoped there might be a nice little trip to Toronto to give evidence, but sadly for them their Witness Statements were accepted by the Defence Counsel uncontested. Shame, they really deserved something for their hard work. But they did have the satisfaction of seeing a job well done.

**

As a postscript to the work of the Tarmac Officers it is necessary to explain how they are able to look in suitcases when the owner isn't present. Firstly, on most occasions they don't actually look in suitcases, they tend to look at them, and feel them, and smell them, pick them up and feel the weight, check to see if they don't stand right, are they unbalanced? Or it may be that they fit a trend, have they seen a similar type with drugs in. All these things may well tell a Customs Officer what he or she wants to know. On occasion however it will be necessary to open the case or bag. Section 159 of the Customs and Excise Management 1979 gives them the power to do this in the presence of a representative of the passenger. It is a power they are very keen not to abuse and whenever humanly possible they will seek to do it in the presence of a member of the airline or a member of British Airports Authority workforce who is deemed at that point to be the representative of the passenger.

**

The JM001 and the BA262

If any flights sum up the Customs battle against the importation of drugs in the learning years it would be the JM 001, Air Jamaica, and the BA262, British Airways. Both the flights from Kingston from Jamaica and Mo Bay, They were mayhem, especially the Air Jamaica. They were like a massive training exercise. You just knew there was something there. Virtually every passenger was carrying something they shouldn't be carrying, even if it was only a plant with earth on its' roots. Every imaginable concealment. Cannabis or cocaine, no heroin. Then in the latter years crack cocaine.

Cannabis inside ginger cakes, inside tins of fruit, inside coconuts. Cannabis oil in the cover of books, cocaine underneath wigs, swallowers all over the place. Cocaine in solution inside factory sealed bottles of rum. On top of all the normal drugs there was 'cannabrum' a mixture of white rum and herbs, many of the herbs were cannabis related. There was gallon after gallon of 'Wray and Nephew' white over-proof rum. There were illegal importations of meat and plants. Dead animals, illegal foodstuffs. You name it, be sure it was found in the passenger's baggage. Customs never actually adopted a "full turn out" policy. A full turn out, as the name suggests, being a flight where everybody is stopped and searched. There would have been riots if they had. Also, although there was no such thing as the Human Rights Act – that delightful piece of legislation didn't appear on the statute books until 1998. There was the European Convention of Human Rights, and accusations of racial discrimination would have been heard from here to Strasbourg and back. So it was managed by placing a couple of officers at the front of the Green Channel. They would ask every passenger coming into the Green how many bottles of rum they had. At least three quarters of them would be in excess of their Duty Free Allowance, so the officers would direct them into the Red Channel. The rest would be allowed into the Green and they would all be stopped. Then, when there were no more passengers to come through the Green, the officers would transfer to the Red and deal with the massive queue waiting in there. It was crude, but it worked. It wasn't a full turn out as such, but virtually every passenger was spoken to and probably searched.

**

Tony, a larger than life character who kept a sheep in his back garden to keep the grass down, was in his element when doing battle with the Jamaicans. Tony had two great loves in his life, Manchester United, and good wine, especially red. But a close third was doing battle with the Jamaicans. He had many good solid jobs that had put numerous offenders behind bars. At his peak he worked on a team led by the previously mentioned Geoff, who was by now a Senior Officer. Tony was a prolific seizing Officer, with many high quality seizures under his belt, but sadly he will always be remembered for one embarrassing incident which would have made a great story in the tabloids.

It was late in 1978, and he was waiting for the JM001. Tony was on the 7 to 3 shift. The 001 had gone a little bit late and it wasn't due until two o'clock in the afternoon. This was perfect for Tony, there would certainly be something on it and it would almost certainly mean overtime, which on a Sunday meant double time. He knew his boss Geoff wouldn't argue about a little bit of overtime. He was in a good mood anyway as his beloved United had won the day before, and he had celebrated with a particularly good bottle of red. Tony liked to stand at the mouth of the Green Channel and watch the passengers as they clustered around the baggage belt in the Reclaim Hall. Customs always made sure that the BAA staff knew to put the JM001 on the belt immediately in front of the Green so they could get a really good look at everyone as they waited for their baggage. As he stood there watching the various bags come up on the carousel he noticed a young man looking around him and looking very nervous.

This was important because Tony would be watching for his body language when he stopped him. Would he still be nervous or would he suddenly become very calm. He picked up a scruffy looking bag. Sure enough he was on his own, another good sign. Drug smugglers were normally on their own.

Tony stopped Mr Winston Phillips. He was a resident in this country and he had been back to Jamaica to visit relatives. This would have been very innocent and there was nothing suspicious in his story. But Tony noticed that Mr Phillips who had seemed very nervous and was looking all over the place in the Reclaim Area before he picked up his bags, was suddenly very calm and relaxed. This, Tony knew was classic drug smuggler behaviour. He knew that Phillips had been preparing himself for the moment he might be stopped. He had been telling himself not to act nervously or guiltily. As a consequence instead of showing all the normal emotions to being stopped; surprise, nerves, outrage, even guilt. Mr Phillips was calm and relaxed. None of the usual, "you've only stopped me because I'm black", which he was half expecting.

Tony searched his baggage and inside a homemade Jamaican ginger cake he found six-hundred grams of cannabis. This was home cooking with a difference. It was the Great British Bake Off but with a bit of added spice. I'm not sure Mary Berry and Paul Hollywood would have approved. There was nothing else unusual. Mr Phillips was duly arrested and interviewed. Unusually he actually admitted knowing it was there and he admitted he knew he was breaking the law by trying to bring it into the country. Difficult to deny if you've actually gone to the trouble of putting it inside a cake. But some will try. Phillips was duly charged and put in the cells overnight. The next day Tony and his witness appeared at Uxbridge Magistrates Court, and presented the facts to the Court. Phillips was brought up before a Magistrates panel that was being chaired by Mrs Lavinia Cox. Now, Mrs Lavinia Cox, had ferocious, reputation especially when dealing with drug smugglers. However on this particular Monday morning she must have been having a good hair day and she duly fined Phillips two-hundred pounds. This was quite a light slap on the wrist. Mrs Cox was happy that it was for personal use. Phillips had been compliant, hadn't caused any trouble, and importantly he had admitted his guilt. Everything was very relaxed. Phillips had relatives there to pay his fine. Tony retuned his passport to him and he returned all the personal possessions that had been detained the previous day, along with his suitcase. Job done. Phillips went off to catch his train from Kings Cross and Tony was on his way back to Terminal Three. A straightforward offence, no dramatics; a bread and butter job. No stress, no aggravation. Even more important because it didn't go to Crown Court, there were no Witness Statements to write. Witness Statements were a real chore. There were so many rules about what could and could not go in them. Officers found them a real minefield.

It was only when Tony had arrived back in the Terminal and he was doing the paper work and putting the job to bed that he noticed that something was missing. In fact something very important was missing. The cannabis was nowhere to be seen! With a sudden flash of clarity Tony remembered that when they were getting ready that morning, to make it easier to carry everything, he had placed the drugs and the cake back in Phillips's suitcase. And there they had remained throughout the Hearing. More importantly, there they had also remained when Tony returned Phillips's personal effects. Unwittingly, he had returned the drugs to Phillips when he returned his suitcase to him. The language was amazing and also the speed with which Tony could move for such a big man. All thoughts of Man United winning on Saturday, about which he was still going on and on, disappeared from his head. Tony and his witness grabbed an official car and were off to Kings Cross. Fortunately they knew Phillips was heading for Liverpool so they knew which platform to look on. Their only hope was that Phillips and his relatives decided to have a celebration drink before boarding it. This they did, so when Tony arrived at Kings Cross Phillips was still there, and so was the cannabis. There ensued a most interesting conversation on the platform.

Tony: Have you had a look in your suitcase?

Phillips: What do you want?

The whole affair had been quite amicable but the last person on earth who Phillips wanted to see at that moment in time was Tony.

Tony: Can we have a look, somewhere a bit quiet?

Phillips: What for man?

Tony: Well there is a distinct possibility that you might be walking around London with 600 grams of herb in your suitcase.

Phillips: You're shitting me man.

Tony: Fraid not.

The suitcase was opened and sure enough there was the heavy plastic bag all neatly sealed up with the drugs still inside.

Phillips went white, well perhaps not white, but very very pale. He had unknowingly been walking around London with 600 grams of the finest Jamaican weed in his suitcase. Had he been stopped by the police and the cannabis had been found absolutely nobody would have believed him when he claimed that HM Customs had given it to him. To celebrate his close shave, Phillips took Tony for a pint - actually Tony had a red wine - before he got on his train. He was sure Tony had done it deliberately, and had done it simply because he knew he supported Liverpool.

Tony's blushes were spared, but his colleagues made sure he never forgot it.

**

Tony was also responsible for highlighting the nonsense that was 'cannabrum'; this being over proof white rum with a variety of herbs in it; some of these herbs would be cannabis, but the amounts were minute, too small to be measured. They didn't mean a prosecution, they were simply seized and reported, but they were still time consuming. People still had to be spoken to, details taken, checks made to see if they were repeat offenders. Tony showed the ridiculous system HM Customs were forced to operate when he stopped a family of 5, all adults, off of the BA262. They were all Jamaican nationals who were coming here to visit relatives. Quite naturally, they were bringing gifts. Jamaican ginger cake, fruit, sweet potatoes, breadfruit. All the things the Jamaicans loved but which at that time you just couldn't get over here in the UK. They were in high spirits and were laughing and joking with Tony, this was very often the way with the Jamaicans on holiday. Sadly, amongst all their baggage were eight bottles of white over proof rum with a sort of pink tinge to them and with various bits of herbage floating around. Tony tested them, and lo and behold they reacted positive to the cannabis field test. He had uncovered eight bottles of 'cannabrum'. This was a pain, but it was no big deal. A quick interview, very, very quick. A few checks then send them on their way. But then things went downhill rapidly. All five members of the family laid claim to at least one bottle. So Tony had five offences to process. In fact he had five joint offences because they all knew what each other were carrying. The net result was Tony called in the team, and five Officers, with five jockey's, processed one offence each. A whole team, ten officers, taken out of action by eight bottles that should have been flushed down the toilet.

**

Mainly the Jamaicans were good natured, even some of them who were involved in drugs. An Officer by the name of Mike: who bore a more than passing resemblance to Alfred E Newman (the comic character from the Mad magazine), and had a sense of humour to match. He had stopped a large Jamaican lady who had numerous pieces of baggage. Mike had opened the largest of them and was confronted by package after package after package. All wrapped in brown paper and tied up with string. Mike proceeded to open them one by one. He just squeezed each one tore a little bit of the brown paper and sniffed.

"What's this?" Mike asks.

"Oh dat's sorrel", says the large lady. Sorrel a herb, no problem.

"What's this?" Asks Mike opening the next package.

"Oh dat's tea bush" comes the reply. Mike smells it. It definitely is tea bush.

On to the next. "What's this?"

"Ginger", she says. The smell is distinctive.

And so it goes on. Then Mike opens another package and immediately the pungent smell of cannabis fills the air. It is so strong that the two officers on the adjoining benches can smell it. They both look at Mike hoping that he might take them in as his jockey. It's a bread and butter offence but they still want to get involved. Nothing with Mike is ever boring. One of them, Paul, moves in a bit closer so that he can corroborate anything that is said from now on. He later admits that this was a mistake.

"What's this?"

This time the lady smells it. "Dat's cat food" she says.

Mike looks at her smells it again. He's wondering just how many cats are vegetarian. "What is it?" He asks again.

"Dat's cat food"

"You have vegetarian cats in Kingston?" Mike says with a soppy grin on his face.

The lady makes no reply.

Mike smells it again, then he gives it to Paul to smell.

Paul smiles and shrugs his shoulders.

"What is it?" He asks for a third time.

"I tell you dat is cat food"

"Well all I can say is that if this is cat food then you must have one f......g happy pussy", says Mike, looking her straight in the eye.

The lady can't believe her ears, and neither can Paul. Although knowing Mike he's not entirely surprised.

"What is dat you say about ma pussy?" Exclaims the Jamaican lady.

"Your cat", said Mike still looking her straight in the eyes. "You must have a very happy cat."

"Oh ma cat", said the lady very slowly and dissolving into laughter.

"What did you think I meant, what other sort of pussy is there", asked Mike?

The lady just shook her head and laughed.

No prizes for guessing what she thought he meant. Also no prizes for guessing what he really did mean.

At Court Paul regretted moving in so close so quickly. He was subjected to a severe roasting by the Defending Counsel because as he was giving his evidence about this conversation he couldn't help smiling. The Defending Counsel didn't think it was a laughing matter. Fortunately the rest of the Court did.

** **

But as time went on the light side of the Jamaican flights was replaced by a darker side. HM Customs started to see more and more cocaine, coke, snow, candy, candy cane, snort, or whatever else it might be called. The 'Yardies' became more and more visible and officers were dealing with more and more hardened criminals.

Wally was in the Green Channel Terminal Three. He wasn't happy the 001 had gone late and he knew that if he did score it would mean an extended shift, and that would definitely mean more trouble at home. The overtime was nice but Wally would rather be at home on a Sunday having lunch with his family, and his Sunday lunchtime pint.

The 001 was the usual mayhem. It was 1981 and it had been a slow period. Results were poor. But this flight was looking promising. There were delays upstairs in Immigration so the passengers were filtering down very slowly. The Tarmac boys were out the back and so were the dogs. There had already been two indications (not yet confirmed but possible) so the bags were also coming through slowly. There was a massive amount of baggage and the aircraft was full to the rafters. It was going to be a long old slog. It was confirmed, the Tarmac boys had a positive. A bag-full. Bag-full being the "technical" term for a suitcase that contained nothing else but drugs. On this occasion and almost every other occasion when it was a bag-full, it was cannabis. The dogs also had a couple of partials. Large bags with lots of packages inside. Without opening up the packages you couldn't be sure, and those packages needed to be opened in front of the punter.

Gradually the Reclaim Hall was filling up. The baggage was piling up on the carousel. A few lucky people were getting their bags and some coming through the Green and some were going through the Red Channel. Most of these early types didn't have much baggage so it wasn't taking long for them to be cleared. Then the pace quickened and suddenly everyone in the Green was occupied. There were six Tarmac officers waiting for the bag-full and the two dog indications. The SO, Mike, a man with a vocabulary to rival the Concise Oxford Dictionary, was at the front of the Green diverting anyone who admitted having more than their allowances into the Red. The queue in the Red was getting longer and longer. Mike was also trying to keep an eye on what was going on in the Green. Everything was extremely noisy.

"You've only stopped me cause ah am black."

Mike looked round to see a black woman being stopped by a black Officer. It always made him smile, especially as 99% of the passengers on the 001 were black. For whatever reason Caucasian people seemed to avoid the JM001. So if you didn't stop black people you didn't stop anyone. Then he was being asked for some advice from an officer who had found what looked like a lot of dead bats. They were all squashed into a suitcase with their mouths gaping open. *Are they a protected species?* The officer wanted to know. If they are, said Mike, it hasn't been very successful.

Every bench was occupied. Some officers had people queuing up, this wasn't strictly correct, but some did it anyway. Wally was right at the end of the Channel. He was dealing with a couple of twenty-somethings. The Jamaican flights tended to be the only flights where the 'drug smugglers travel alone', law didn't apply. He was losing interest and he was looking at anyone else walking down the Channel. He would keep trying with these two until something better came along. He was almost finished when he spotted a man weaving his way down the Channel. Somehow he had walked straight past Mike and hadn't been stopped by any of the other officers, probably because they all had their heads down in suitcases. He was wearing jeans and a bomber jacket and he was pushing a trolley on which he had two hard sided brown suitcases. In those days it was relatively unusual to see hard sided suitcases coming from the West Indies. Wally was very interested. He let him get almost past him, and as he was the last officer in the Channel he would have been out, then he stepped out and asked him to bring his trolley to the bench. He deliberately left it late before he moved because he wanted to see if the man, having thought he was through, displayed any reaction to being stopped. But no, Leroy Winston Montereaux was as cool as the proverbial cucumber.

Wally was sure that Mr Montereaux was up to something from the word go. He was too relaxed, too calm. He fitted the profile perfectly. Travelling alone, third time he had travelled this year, none of the usual bits and pieces associated with Jamaicans who live here and have been back to Kingston or Mo Bay to see the family. Only one bottle of rum, none of the usual packets and parcels containing all sorts of herbs and spices. No bottles containing dubious looking concoctions of a whole variety of liquids and herbs. He was a barman in a club in Manchester, but somehow he had managed to afford three trips back to Jamaica in less than 6 months. It got worse, or better, when Wally looked at the ticket.

Cash paid! Drug smugglers and the organisations they worked for only dealt in cash; no audit trails with cash. Leroy lifted the first suitcase on the bench and opened it. Clothing, shoes, toiletries, nothing odd there. As he was looking through the case Wally found a reason to move the suitcase, ostensibly to help him reach the contents on the far side of it, but in reality to judge the weight. This told him all he needed to know. It was too heavy, and even when it was laying on the bench it didn't feel balanced. More than this though, it was the worst concealment of its type that Wally had ever seen. The lining of the suitcases had been simply peeled back, the drugs placed underneath and the lining glued back down. However in his efforts not to get glue on the lining, Montereaux, or whoever actually concealed the cocaine, hadn't put enough glue under the lining and it was actually turning up at the edges. He was now as sure as he could be that he was dealing with a commercial consignment concealed inside a false top and bottom of the suitcase. He knew there could be up to twenty kilos of cocaine in the two suitcases. This would make it well worth letting it run to see where it might lead.

Wally asked Mike, the same Mike who was dealing with the woman who owned a cannabis eating cat, and was one of his team, to check out the Passport. Leroy smiled and said, "You might find I've been a naughty boy in the past." He wasn't joking. Mike came back with some worrying information. Winston had already been inside twice in this country for knife crime. Other information told us that he was a connected 'Yardie' in Manchester. If he was a barman at all it was only part time. His main job was as an enforcer for one of the Manchester gangs. Despite this information Mike, the SO not the cannabis cat Mike, took the decision to let it run. He was probably heading for Manchester, but as he had no rail tickets and he was very vague about his movements, there was just a chance that someone might be meeting him by car.

While Wally was taking his time looking through the baggage, Terry, (sometimes called Welly as a reference to a picture of the top of his head that made him look like a combination of the actor Telly Savalas and a wellington boot), one of the local Investigation Team who we have seen previously in this book, briefed a dozen officers in civvies. The main essence of his briefing was, "Nobody takes any unnecessary risks". He knew this was the heavy mob and he wasn't taking any chances.

The men were in place. Wally let Leroy Winston proceed. He obviously knew his way around, well he had been through Terminal Three at least twice in the recent past. He went to Smiths, bought a newspaper and then headed straight for the Underground. This brought the run to an abrupt conclusion. The Underground is too dangerous, it's too easy to lose a target, and innocent people can get hurt. If somebody as large and apparently violent as Montereaux decided to fight, it could be extremely dangerous not just for the officers but for anyone near him. It was a shame because he only had enough money to get into central London, he was certainly being met there. Six officers closed in on Montereaux and this was when he showed his true colours. As soon as he saw what was happening he abandoned his trolley with the suitcases on it and literally made a run for it. As Customs were in front of him as well as coming up from behind he was soon brought down by an officer who went by the name of Ollie; a would be rugby player. There was an almighty struggle, eventually Montereaux was handcuffed. This still didn't stop him, he still tried to run for it even though he had his hands handcuffed behind his back. In the end two officers sat on him, face down on a tiled floor. They just sat on him for two or three minutes while it finally percolated through to him that he wasn't going anywhere. But even then as he was marched back to the Customs Hall he struggled so much that they had to carry him. As they carried him he was bucking and throwing himself around like a fish or a seal on dry land trying to get back in the water. During this pantomime Leroy continued to verbally abuse the officers. They were all told that he remembered their faces and when he was free he and his mates would be visiting them and their families, and it wouldn't be a social call. He fixed one Officer with a horrible stare and told him.

"OK I do Strangeways but when I's out I come see you, see you, yes you. I come see you."

This was all very intimidating but it was also very useful to Wally. Montereaux had been arrested and Cautioned that he was not obliged to say anything unless he wished to do so. But anything he did say may be written down and given in evidence. As a consequence his rantings about what he was going to do when he got out of prison amounted to admission that he had been up to something. It was going to make it very difficult him to deny all knowledge of the drugs. As this was the usual excuse it was, to say the least, very useful to Wally in the interview.

The interview and investigation proved much less problematical than the arrest. Although he continued to make threats against Wally, against who he seemed to have an almost pathological dislike. He seemed to feel he had been tricked and that this wasn't right. It was alright for him to smuggle large amounts of cocaine, but it was all wrong when the devious Customs Officer pretended he hadn't found the drugs when in fact he knew they were there all along. His view on what was right and wrong in life was truly astounding.

The concealment was duly opened in front of Montereaux who went through the usual theatrics of feigning surprise and asking what it was. This beggared the question, just what did he think he was going to prison for if he didn't know he was carrying something illegal? There were nine kilos of cocaine in each suitcase.

The interview was bizarre. Montereaux answered many of the questions as if he was talking about a third person:-

Wally: "Can you explain why you have been to Jamaica so many times in such a short period of time?"

Montereaux: "Leroy, says he just feel like it"

Wally: "Do you mean you just felt like it?"

Montereaux: "Leroy, he just feel like it, so he go"

Or when asked how he was going to get back to Manchester with virtually no money.

Montereaux: "Leroy he don't tink he wanna answer dat one."

Wally of course then had to explain to the tape recorder that Montereaux was speaking about himself. He also took the unusual step of involving the Solicitor to confirm that there were only four people in the room. There wasn't another defendant, only Leroy Winston Montereaux.

When he was asked exactly what he thought he was going to prison for if he had no knowledge of the drugs, Montereaux replied:

"Leroy has already been fitted two times before."

Sometimes he would just say:

"No I don't tink Leroy he wanna answer dat one, no don't tink so, no".

At one point a muffled voice could be heard on the tape.

"Sounds like he's having an out of body experience."

It wasn't Wally and it wasn't Mike. No, it was the Solicitor. Who obviously found this bizarre interview as confusing as the two Officers.

After the Solicitor had arrived for the interview, Montereaux had stayed calm, although his ankle was handcuffed to the chair he was sitting on and all the chairs in the Interview Rooms are bolted to the floor. This is not because Customs were frightened the chairs might be stolen. It was to remove the temptation the prisoner might have to place the chair lovingly over the officer's head. The officer's chairs were also bolted to the floor and this was for the same reason. A particularly stupid answer really could make one feel like hitting the moron opposite with anything that came to hand. A chair would do nicely.

Leroy made no admissions but the circumstantial evidence was overwhelming. On top of that, and this was very rare in those days, finger print evidence was obtained which showed Leroy had handled the packages. Despite the normal number of, "no reply" answers to all the crunch questions, the twelve just men duly found him guilty and he was eventually invited to spend the next twelve years in Her Majesty's Prison, Strangeways.

As the trial progressed he became more and more threatening towards the prosecution witnesses, especially to Wally. It was so bad that Judge Murchie called a halt to the proceedings on three separate occasions. Judge Murchie was a Judge much loved and admired by Customs Officers. He ruled his court with a rod of iron. But at the same time he was very fair. He also hated drug smugglers and wouldn't let the defending Counsel get away with any of the usual rubbish they threw at the officers. At the end of the trial the members of jury were discharged and told they would be excused jury service for life as it had been such a harrowing experience for them. At times Leroy was threatening them individually:

"You in de red dress, yeh you look away, but I got your face, I come and see you when I get out."

The only moment of levity came when the Defending Barrister was building up to giving Mike a hard time over the "Out of body" remark. The Solicitor could be seen desperately trying to catch the Barristers' eye. Judge Murchie realised something was amiss and told the Barrister his Solicitor was trying to catch his attention. There was a muttered conversation between the two. Then, refreshingly, the Barrister informed Judge Murchie that he had been barking up the wrong tree. The Judge wasn't happy with that and the Barrister had to admit that it was indeed the Defending Solicitor who was responsible for the out of body remark. It was one of those very rare moments in a trial involving drugs that Judge Murchie actually smiled.

Then he, that is Montereaux not Judge Murchie, calmed down for a while, but when the verdict was announced his real vicious character came back to the surface. As he was taken down he was issuing the same threats to the members of the jury that he had made to Wally and the arresting officers. In particular the next day when they came back for sentencing he was screaming at Wally, who was sat next to the Prosecuting Counsel. He kept telling him:-

"I got your face, I got your face, and I got your voice".

Wally assumed that he meant he could change his appearance but unless he changed his voice he would still be able to recognise him from his dulcet East London tones. Montereaux was obviously still very upset that Wally had tricked him. It was after this case that Wally developed the nervous habit of continually looking back over his left shoulder. In fact, that Christmas, a short time after the trial, he was at a pantomime with his children when the Ugly Sisters suddenly shouted, "he's behind you," Much to the amazement of his children Wally prostrated himself on the floor..

Leroy Winston Montereaux, despite his flamboyant, artistic, almost comical name, really did represent the dark side of the drugs industry.

**

Concealments become more devious

The drug smuggler not only tried different ways of avoiding Customs altogether, they also became more and more devious in the concealments they would try. Eventually they would arrive at the ultimate hiding place. The internal concealment. That is the swallower. But before and after the swallowers came on the scene they would still try to find the perfect concealment. The concealment that would be undetectable even if the mule was stopped. Some of these concealments will be discussed in other chapters of this book. The double sided or double top and bottom to a suitcase, the saturated clothing or carpets will come later, but some are only appropriate to this chapter because of their deviousness.

**

Frank, another 'Scouser', was watching the British West Indian Airways (BWI, pronounced B-wee) flight from Port of Spain come through the Green Channel in Terminal Three. He was looking for people, and in particular women, travelling alone. He was focusing on black women because recently there had been a rash of black women carrying half a kilo of cocaine under wigs that were sewn into their natural head of hair. These wigs were sewn onto the natural hair so, to quote Ernie Wise, "you couldn't see the join."

As he stood there at the mouth of the Green watching the passengers milling around the Baggage Belt he noticed two white women who looked to be in their late twenties or early thirties; and who just didn't look right. In fact they not only didn't look right, they looked extremely wrong. For one thing they were white, and the B-wee catered mainly for West Indians. Secondly most of the white people who were on the B-wee were holiday makers, and these two girls certainly didn't look like holiday makers. They weren't dressed like young women who'd been on holiday. They didn't have a tan. They weren't wearing the usual; casual shoes, cut down trousers or loose skirt and a casual lightweight top. No, they were wearing high heeled stiletto shoes, short, very tight skirts, and long sleeved tops with plunging neck lines. Most young women coming from the West Indies wear their hair in a very casual style, or maybe braided, and they wear almost no make-up. These two girls had their hair done up on top of their heads with loads of lacquer, and the make-up was plastered on thick enough to sink a battleship. One of them was chewing. Not nervously, just chewing and chewing. Frank decided they looked like they were on the game. And he was dead right. He found out later that they were both prostitutes from Sheffield. At the time he said they would have looked much more at home if they'd had a lamp post to lean against.

The only thing that worried him was that they were obviously travelling together. In his experience drug smugglers travelled alone. Well, nine times out of ten they did. Despite this he decided they were worth a tug.

He called them over to the bench. There were none of the silly jokes or strange nervous behaviour that he expected from people who've got nothing to hide. But they weren't exactly calm either. Not the calm of the drug smuggler who has been saying to him or herself, "If I'm stopped I'm going to act calm. I'm not going to act guilty or nervous". No he described them as being very, "focused". As if they were concentrating very hard on something. Their story was that they had been on holiday for two weeks, and indeed their airline tickets confirmed that they had jetted out two weeks previously. It also showed Frank that they had paid cash for the tickets. Another good sign, as you know by now drugs organisations prefer to deal in cash. They gave the name of the hotel as the Hilton. They didn't have a receipt from the hotel or any other proof of having stayed there. They did have some cocktail sticks with the word Hilton engraved into the plastic, and one of them showed Frank a linen serviette that she "borrowed" from the Hotel dining room. But Frank figured they could have got them if they'd simply gone there for a drink, or had lunch. It was all looking more and more dodgy.

He asked them what they'd done during their two weeks. "Just lying round the pool." was the reply. Frank commented on their lack of sun tans, but they said they were frightened of getting burnt so they stayed under cover most of the time. Frank was wondering if they'd been doing a bit of free-lance work out there. You don't get much of a tan if you're on your back all night and sleeping all day.

They said they did bar work in Sheffield and mentioned a couple of local bars. "How did you afford a holiday like this if all you do is bar work," Frank asked? "The tips are good and we've been saving for a long time", came the reply.

Frank searched the baggage, but without result. He searched their hand baggage and although the Customs seals were intact, he even looked in two Duty Free Boxes they were carrying. But apart from the fact that they were a little over their alcohol allowance (each box contained two three quarter litre bottles of rum, so they were both half a litre in excess), he found nothing. He then had the girls strip searched. Again without result. While this search was going on he made one or two telephone calls and very soon he had it confirmed that they were prostitutes from the Sheffield area with a string of minor convictions against their names. He was again thinking that maybe they had an offer to go and work in the clubs in Port of Spain. Surprisingly, white prostitutes could earn very good money out there. Novelty value perhaps. Or maybe they were swallowers! We hadn't seen a lot of swallowers at this time but we were aware of them. Frank didn't think they were swallowers. He decided to go through the suitcases again, and this time he involved a second Officer by the name of Des just in case he was missing the "bleedin obvious". No, there was nothing. He looked at the hand baggage for a second time and the Duty Free boxes. Nothing. He even looked at the bottles of rum, but they were all commercially intact.

The young women had been in the Green Channel with Frank for about forty five minutes but they weren't showing any signs of irritation or really questioning what the problem was. This could have been because of their profession, of course. They were probably used to being questioned and searched and being made to wait for no good reason. But Frank was getting desperate. He had a little chat with them about swallowing drugs, and they appeared to genuinely not have a clue what he was talking about. He had to explain it in words of one syllable. They were incredulous and vehemently denied having swallowed any packages. When Frank explained that the drugs were normally wrapped in condoms (this would change over the years) one did say that she could make more money out of using condoms in a quite different way. Although they still maintained they worked in a bar Frank realised that was what they meant when they said that the tips were good.

The only thing in the baggage that had come from Port of Spain was the Duty Free Box and the rum. The suitcases were old and there were no false sides or top or bottom. Everything in the suitcases and the hand baggage had come from the UK except for some small items such as the cocktail sticks. But nothing that could contain or be made of cocaine or cannabis. So if they weren't swallowers and they hadn't been on a working holiday, it had to be something to do with the Duty Free rum or the box the rum was in.

He cut the box, in fact he destroyed both boxes to make absolutely sure, but it was all cardboard, no secret compartments. He crumbled some of the cardboard and tested it for cocaine and cannabis. Negative. He looked at the bottles but they were definitely commercially intact. There was no doubt that they had been sealed in a bottling plant. He inspected the bottles again. The rum was the lovely gold colour of West Indian rum. There were no false bottoms in the bottles. Then, and he could never explain why, he decided to open one of the bottles and test the rum for cocaine. We had seen cannabis oil, that is liquid cannabis, but it was very thick. This rum had the same consistency of rum, it didn't however have the beautiful smell associated with the golden liquid. Frank dropped a few drops on to the filter paper. Then he added a few drops of the reagent. Eureka! He couldn't believe his eyes when he saw it turn a lovely blue colour. This was a positive reaction to the cocaine field test. Frank had just discovered the first known importation of cocaine in solution. For a while it would become quite common, but this was the first. On the 20th of May 2009 at Croydon Crown Court, the England cricketer Chris Lewis would be sentenced to thirteen years in prison for bringing in 3.37 kilograms of liquid cocaine inside tins of fruit. But Frank was the first, and it was all because the two young women, "just didn't look right for the flight they were on. "

Altogether there was half a kilo of cocaine in each bottle. The girls of course denied all knowledge of the cocaine. When they finally arrived in Isleworth Crown Court, Frank had to admit to the jury that. "Yes, the Duty Free Box seal was intact. And yes, there were no signs that the box had been tampered. And he had to agree that the bottles were commercially sealed and the seal hadn't been broken." On top of that he had to agree that the bottles did look like they had been sealed in a factory. Although he did add the caveat that he wasn't an expert on how bottles are sealed in bottling plants. He was quite good at opening them but that's another matter. All of this was good for the ladies claim that they had no knowledge of the contents of the bottles. They thought it was rum. However, what was bad was everything else. Where was the DFS receipt for the rum? What exactly had they been doing in Port of Spain? Inquiries established that they hadn't stayed at the Hilton. So where had they stayed, and why had they lied? Surprisingly they never used the excuse that might have swayed the jury. That is that they were "working girls" taking a working holiday. Maybe they felt that this would prejudice the jury against them. The jury duly found them both guilty, and they were sentenced to five and a half years each.

What this showed to Customs was not only how devious the concealments were becoming. It also showed how much better the organised the gangs they were battling against had become. They obviously now had contacts in both the bottling plants, and even more worryingly, the Duty Free Shops. Which were, and are, under the control of the local Customs.

**

Olatunde Adibe was a business man from Lagos. He'd been back and forth between London and Lagos on several occasions. On this trip he was unlucky enough to bump into an Officer who we will call Des.

Des was watching the BA from Lagos as it made its' way through the Green Channel in Terminal Three. Not the actual flight, you understand, just the passengers who had arrived on it. It was the usual hotchpotch of passengers. Mostly Nigerians, but a few white faces in amongst the crowd. Des was actually concentrating more on the whites rather than the IC3s; that is, rather than the Afro-Caribbeans. There had been a recent spate of single white males coming from Nigeria and Ghana carrying heroin in suitcases with false tops and bottoms. This trend would carry on for several months. Des wasn't having much luck. Everyone he stopped who fitted the profile of this latest trend appeared to be very genuine businessmen. Then, as the flight was beginning to thin out, he spotted the man he would later find out was Mr Olatunde Adibe. He wasn't white, he was Nigerian. He had a baggage trolley absolutely piled high with baggage. He looked like a businessman, but he looked a bit shabby. His suit looked a bit tired, his shoes needed a clean, his shirt looked a bit grubby, and his tie wasn't knotted properly.

Des stopped him, called him over to the bench. His reaction wasn't classic drug smuggler. He laughed.

"Ah! Oh no not again. Every time I get stopped. I must have a guilty face."

Des didn't like to agree with him so he just went into the normal questioning. He had a good story. He was a businessman. He was genuinely here on business. He supplied parts for office equipment in Nigeria. He was over here to speak to his suppliers and to pick up some high value parts that he didn't trust going through the systems in Lagos. And who could blame him for that? He could show three or four apparently genuine meetings in his diary. He could also show lists of parts he would be ordering. He had a hotel booking for seven days. This was the first moment of disquiet that Des felt. The hotel was in the Seven Sisters Road, Finsbury Park, North London, and it was known to Customs and Police as a favourite location for a whole variety of nefarious goings on. It was certainly on the HM Customs and Excise suspect list, and Des knew this. He had a small amount of cash but no credit cards. The two star hotel was going to cost peanuts, but how would he pay for the parts? Mr Adibe apparently had an account with the supplier.

Des decided to do the bags. The flight was almost finished, just a few stragglers. Nobody had got anything, not a sniff. Des asked him if he'd packed the bags himself. Adibe said he had. Des asked him if he was carrying anything for anyone else. Adibe said he wasn't. Des asked these questions while the bags were still on the trolley. He did this because very often the passenger would still think they could lie their way through. Later these two statements would be Adibes' undoing. In total there were five pieces of baggage. A large soft sided suitcase. A large red holdall and a small black holdall with gold stripes down the side. A cardboard box tied up with string and a shoulder bag.

Des started with the large suitcase. Nothing. He then went on to the red holdall. Nothing. Then the black holdall with gold stripes. Still nothing. The flight had finished and there was nothing in the Reclaim Hall so Des carried on even though he didn't fancy Mr Adibe very much by now. He untied the cardboard box and found it to be full of twenty coconuts. Mr Adibe said he was bringing them for someone here. Now this was where it began to unravel a little bit. Adibe had previously stated that he'd packed the bags himself and that he wasn't carrying anything for anyone else. It now turned out that although he knew the box was full of coconuts, he hadn't packed it and he was carrying something for someone else. Bringing in coconuts might seem a bit strange and suspicious to the reader but people really do carry the strangest things and coconuts were actually quite common. They were more common coming from the Caribbean but West Africa wasn't unheard of. So it wasn't the coconut that alerted Des, it was the change of story.

Des looked at the coconuts, shook a few of them, yes he could hear the milk, and at first they all seemed to be intact with no sign of tampering. Having confirmed with Adibe that the box had been packed by a certain Mr X of Lagos and that he, Adibe, had had nothing to do with them at all, Des moved on to the shoulder bag. Nothing in it of interest, except a small ball of plastic string. Exactly the same as the string that had been used to tie up the box. Adibe claimed he had used it to tie up the box. Later under caution in the interview Des asked him if the box had been undone when Mr X gave it to him. Realising the position he was in if he agreed that it was, he changed this and claimed that the mysterious Mr X had given it to him in case he felt the box needed more string. Please excuse the pun, but the story seemed to be unravelling just like a roll of string.

Des now returned to the coconuts and he now brought in his witness who we will call Jerry. Jerry picked up the coconuts one by one and shook them. Could he hear the milk inside? Yes he could. Then between them they carried out a much closer inspection of the coconuts. This revealed that six of them had very faint lines down them which you could only see by moving away the fibre. Jerry very gently hit one of the six with a hammer and chisel. It very neatly split into two halves revealing a small package wrapped in back plastic. When this was removed there was a clear plastic bag containing a white powder. In fact it was an unusually white powder. There was half a kilo of heroin at 90% purity in all six coconuts, the very high purity was why it looked so white. So there were three kilos in all. Depending on how much this was cut, and it could be down to as little as 10% per fix, this could be worth as much as five-hundred thousand pounds on the street. What was also interesting were the little plastic phials containing water that had been placed in each coconut. These accounted for the sound of "milk" as Des and Jerry shook them.

Adibe was duly Custodised and put into an Interview Room. He was volubly maintaining his innocence when the Custody officer offered him a Solicitor he said he wanted one. This was a nuisance to Des and Jerry because it slowed things up a bit. It did eventually turn out to be a blessing in disguise, but more of that later. He was refused the right to contact someone else to inform them of his arrest. This was because there was still a possibility that further investigations would need to be made. For example, search of premises could be compromised if the persons waiting for the drugs knew Adibe had been arrested.

The interview took place and was tape recorded. Adibe maintained that the coconuts weren't his. He continued with his story that Mr X had given them to him to give to someone who lived in the UK. He hadn't questioned Mr X. He was quite happy that he was a genuine person. He didn't know the name of the person who they were for. He had simply been told that someone would come to his hotel and ask for his coconuts. He didn't need to know the name, he maintained. Only the person they were for would know he had them and where he was. This was difficult to dispute. The chances of another person just happening to knock on his hotel door and saying, "Don't suppose you've got a box of coconuts from Nigeria", were pretty remote.

Des had switched off the tape recorder and the interview was suspended for a cup of tea. He was looking through his papers and Jerry was looking at one of the unopened coconuts he was looking at the join which was so well disguised it was difficult to see, even though Jerry knew it was there. Jerry then said in a loud voice, but almost as if he was speaking to himself:-

"I wonder how they manage to get such a neat cut. You can hardly see the join."

At this point, Adibe, quite unprompted turned toward Jerry and told him:-

"You put the coconut in a vice so it don't move. Then you get a very fine hack saw blade, you move the fibre to one side and very very carefully you."

He never finished his sentence. He caught sight of the look of horror on his Solicitors face and shut up like a clam. This wasn't on tape, but he was under caution. "Anything you say may be given in evidence etc." So Des and Jerry quickly put it into their Notebooks. The tape was turned back on and Adibe was asked how he knew so much about cutting coconuts in half. He then denied saying it. Even though it was in the Notebooks and he had seen it being written down. The Solicitor was in an embarrassing position. If Adibe disputed that he'd said it he, the Solicitor, could be called as witness for the Prosecution. Fortunately for him after a short discussion with his client he changed his mind. But when asked about it on the tape recorder he said he was just talking about it in general terms he wasn't talking about this particular batch. He knew nothing about them. It must be something that he had read or somebody had told him, or he'd seen on the news. Maybe overheard on a bus or in a bar.

However it made very good evidence for the case for the prosecution. When Des had been questioning him about his knowledge of the prohibition. Adibe had been denying any involvement or knowledge about heroin or any drugs. He had never come into contact with anybody who had any knowledge or involvement with heroin. He had never read anything about drugs. Nobody he knew had any knowledge about drugs. He had never seen or heard anything about any drugs in his whole life. These were pretty incredible statements bearing in mind that he lived in Lagos, and Nigeria was literally awash with heroin at the time and drugs made the national newspapers on a daily basis. So one minute he's the only Nigerian out of a population of over one-hundred million adults who knows absolutely nothing about drugs. The next he's explaining the sophisticated method of cutting open a coconut in order to conceal heroin. It isn't concrete evidence but by showing his knowledge of part of the process he had proved himself an out-and-out liar and this would not go down well with the jury. He of course hadn't been lying when he made those statements. No, he was just confused!

Eventually Olatunde Adibe reached Isleworth Crown Court. The information about the comments made off of the tape recorder were included in the Witness Statements and the Defence did not dispute them. He was tried and found guilty of the attempted evasion of the Prohibition and he was sentenced to eight years locked away from the world.

**

It was a Saturday evening and an Officer: who we will call Malc was off on the Sunday. For some strange reason: probably "sods law"; bad things, by which I mean time consuming things, always came along on the day before your rest day. For a lot of officers this was a good thing because it meant overtime, but for Malc it was bad because he actually appreciated time with his family more than the overtime. In a lot of Officer's eyes this made him a bit odd.

Malc, a Spurs supporter, was in a good mood. His team had won away West Ham and he was looking forward to his Sunday off. Read the Sunday papers, go and watch his eldest lad play football, a couple of pints down the pub, then a Sunday roast. He was looking forward to it as he'd just done three Sundays on the trot. So there he was stood at the mouth of the Green Channel, watching the end of the WT, that is the Nigerian Airways flight from Lagos. There was only one passenger left in the Reclaim Hall, and the rest of the team had disappeared to get on with whatever they were doing, probably not a lot, he thought. There was the one passenger, who he later found out to be Catherine Madeke, and amongst half a dozen suitcases, one enormous grey suitcase going round and round on the belt. He watched her for a while to see if she would claim the suitcase, and she was obviously watching him, waiting for him to go. She could obviously see her suitcase or maybe, suitcases, otherwise she would have trotted off to the airline desk to report a lost bag. Eventually the Officer cracked, he had wanted her to pick up her suitcase to make sure she couldn't claim later it wasn't her suitcase, but he wasn't prepared to hang around all night. He went over to her, stopped the Reclaim Belt, and asked to see her ticket. On it was a baggage tag that matched the one on the suitcase, he also noticed that the ticket was cash paid. This was another good sign for Malc but it wasn't looking too good for Catherine. She agreed it was her suitcase which made the Officer wonder why she had been so reluctant to pick it up while he was watching her. They loaded it onto a trolley and wheeled it into the Green Channel. With a lot of effort he managed to get the suitcase, which weighed forty five kilos, onto the bench. It was no wonder he had a bad back in later years. A few questions established that Catherine was a Nigerian subject coming from Lagos to stay here for a few days. The purpose of her visit was unclear and she wasn't sure where she was going to stay. This was looking worse and worse for Catherine. So far she matched the perfect profile of a drug smuggler. He asked her the usual questions about the contents of the suitcase and she was vague, she was also unsure about whether or not she was carrying anything for anyone. She didn't appear concerned, she was a little aggressive a little confrontational but in the Officer's experience this wasn't unusual when dealing with Nigerian women of a certain age.

"You've only stop me cause I is black," she claimed.

In fact she was the only passenger in the Baggage Hall at the time, so his choice of colour was extremely limited. It would have been impossible to stop someone who wasn't black.

He decided he wasn't going to get any more out of her, so the suitcase was opened. Only to reveal, that apparently it was full of bananas. Nothing else, no clothes, no toiletries, no gifts, nothing but bananas. A little bit perplexed, although not overly so. During his career he had already seen cases full of dead monkeys and dead bats. So nothing would surprise him too much. But because of his surprise all he could think to say was:-

"Oh bananas."

Not very original but he really couldn't think of anything else to say, as all he could see was black, slightly rotten bananas. However he soon found out he was wrong.

"No dey plantains," Catherine replied.

To the uninitiated we are talking about bananas which are smaller, tend to be curly and can be eaten raw, and big straight plantains, which although they are also a fruit of the same genus, need to be cooked. These were the latter. This was a fact that Catherine repeated at least once every five minutes for the next twenty four hours.

So a suitcase full of black rotten plantains. At this point Geoff the SO appeared over his shoulder.

"Get your knife into them" he said stating the bleeding obvious.

This the Officer did, and amazingly instead of going through them like a knife through butter, the knife went about an eighth of an inch and stopped. Luckily Customs Officers were issued with lock knives, otherwise Malc might have been a couple of fingers short. Possession of lock knives is illegal, although bizarrely selling them isn't. But Customs Officers have a dispensation to carry them. Further inspection showed that each banana, sorry, plantain, had been carefully sliced open down one seam. The flesh had been scooped out, filled with compressed herbal cannabis, then the seam sewn together, put into bunches with the stitching on the inside. They were then allowed to rot and go a little bit black. When all the cannabis was removed there was a total of forty- two kilos of cannabis in the suitcase. This was, at this time, a record for weight of drugs in a single suitcase, and probably it still is. You don't see many suitcases that can actually hold forty kilos of anything. It also made the BBC Television 10 o'clock News as Customs were working to rule at the time and there was a lot of publicity about Customs Officers letting drugs flood into the country. The Trade Union made sure the media were aware that this wasn't quite true, and the BBC duly reported it. There were of course a lot of unkind comments from his colleagues about Malc not working to rule because he didn't know the rules anyway.

Anyway, back to Catherine. She had obviously been told that as long as she denied all knowledge of the contents of the bananas, sorry, plantains, Customs couldn't put her in jail. What made Malc think she had been told this? I hear you ask. Well between 20.00 hours on the Saturday and 20.00 hours on the Sunday when she was eventually charged, her answer to almost every pertinent question was:-

"You cannot lock me up."

Questions such as.

"Why didn't you pick up your suitcase when it was the only one left on carousel?"

"You cannot lock me up."

"Why are you bringing a suitcase full of rotten bananas, sorry, plantains to the United Kingdom?"

"You cannot lock me up."

"Who are they for?"

"You cannot lock me up."

"Where are you going with them?"

"You cannot lock me up."

"Why when asked about the contents of the suitcase, didn't you tell me it was full of plantains?"

"You cannot lock me up."

"Where are your clothes?"

"You cannot lock me up."

"How did you get the money to pay for your ticket?"

Straight out every time. "You cannot lock me up."

Questions such as, "where do you live?" "Which flight were you on today?" She answered fully. But anything that might incriminate her in any way at all. Straight back, "You cannot lock me up."

At one point, Joe, a young Irish Officer who was the jockey on this occasion, lent across and in his lilting Irish accent said "Look he's going to lock you up whatever you say, so just answer the bloody questions will ya."

Strictly speaking he was quite correct, but it didn't work. It did of course give the Defence something which they could bring up as intimidation when the Case finally reached Crown Court.

Even as the Officers took her to the North Side Police Station for charging, she was still telling the Custody Sergeant, "You cannot lock me up." The Custody Sergeant looked at her in amazement, as if to say. "What the bloody hell do you think I'm going to do? This is a Custody Suite full of cells, just made for locking people up. Read my job description. I lock people up."

Malc was actually quite worried that when she finally realised she was locked up and that this wasn't some kind of game to get her to confess, she would go berserk and could harm herself. She was stood in the middle of her cell talking to the small observation window.

"You cannot lock me up."

He left the microphone on so she could be heard. He told the Custody Sergeant what he had done and why. Actually he didn't need to tell him he'd left it on because Catherine's dulcet tones could be heard all throughout the Custody Suite.

"You cannot lock me up, you cannot lock me up."

Malc got home about one in the morning. His dinner was in the dog. Six hours later Malc and Joe returned to the Custody Suite to transport Catherine to Uxbridge Magistrates Court. It being necessary to present the evidence before the Magistrates to prove there was sufficient evidence to detain her until Customs were ready to have her Committed for trial at Crown Court. The Custody Sergeant, incandescent with rage by this time nodded at the cells and said.

 "Can you hear that?"

The Nick was heaving, and the noise what deafening; it was Monday morning and every prisoner who had been banged up since Friday evening was being taken to Uxbridge. It was mayhem. The Sergeant quietened everyone down. Yes, you've guessed. There it was.

"You cannot lock me up", very faint, but still audible.

"Now you have my permission to jump the queue, but get her out of my cells pronto, or you'll be taking me before the Magistrate for something a lot more serious than drug smuggling."

This from a very red faced, very unhappy, Custody Sergeant. Apparently Catherine hadn't stopped all night.

The sad thing is that in the end Catherine was spot on. She appeared at Reading Crown Court, Artillery House, the foreman of the jury was a Rastafarian gentleman, and she was found NOT GUILTY. Why Customs Prosecuting Counsel failed to dispute the foremans' inclusion on the jury we will never know. The Rastafarian religion encompasses the spiritual, use of cannabis, their words not mine. He was obviously going to feel she was entitled to import the 42 kilos, so she had committed no crime. However, she was travelling to the UK for no apparent reason with forty two kilos of cannabis concealed in rotten plantains. She couldn't or wouldn't say where she was going or who she was meeting. She didn't have a hotel booking, she had no money, and she had no credit cards, she was unemployed, not a crime, but how did she afford the ticket. She couldn't explain why she didn't pick up her case when it was the only case on the belt and it was so very distinctive. The Officers were probably a little prejudiced, but they had a strong feeling that the jury might have got this one wrong.

Malcolm and Joe couldn't bring themselves to look at Catherine as she left the dock but they suspected she was still mouthing in their direction.

"You cannot lock me up, you cannot lock me up" or maybe she had changed it slightly.

"I told you, you couldn't lock me up."

Although she was released, so technically she was innocent, she was deported and declared "personae non gratae." Amazingly, she never appealed against this ruling.

**

Two Officers who we'll call Tim and Brian were walking back down the Green Channel in Terminal Four. They'd just been for breakfast and they were deep in conversation about the latest Test Match against the West Indies. Holding, Marshall, Ambrose, and Croft were doing their usual thing and knocking back English wickets for fun. They weren't happy.

As they walked past one of the Search Boxes they heard a yelp and looked up to see a black lump flying over the top of the Search Box. It landed on the floor in front of them with a thump. There was a bit of an undignified scramble to get hold of it first. After all Customs Officers are Civil Servants, and Civil Servants are on Performance Related Pay. Tim got to it first, showed it to Brian and they agreed it was a wig with what looked like a small bag of flour sewn into it. Tim banged on the door of the search Box and after a short delay the door was opened. The sight that greeted him was like something out of a second rate gangster movie. There were two lady officers in the room looking very worried and a passenger who looked like she had been beaten up. She had blood running down her face and onto her shoulders and clothing. She was in tears and was holding her face in her hands.

This lady, it transpired, had been stopped by a male Officer, we'll call him Wicks, she had been evasive and hadn't answered any of Wicks's questions properly. She'd arrived on the BA 262 from Kingston Jamaica, so the Officer immediately suspected that she might have some cannabis in her baggage. As he started to search her baggage Miss Hairdo became very angry and confrontational. He was accused of only stopping her because she was black. Now where have we heard that before? He was also subject to a lot of abuse. Now this wasn't unusual, but what was strange was that none of it appeared to be real. Miss Hairdo was making lots of angry noises and saying lots of angry words. But she didn't really seem to be angry. It was as if she was putting on an act. This made Wicksy suspicious in two ways. Firstly, was this a diversion, to distract the other officers in the Green Channel? Indeed was it to distract the Officers in the Red Channel? It could have been as she was making enough noise to be heard in the General Office which was about 100 feet away with several walls in between. So yes, everybody could hear her.

Second, and most likely, was she doing this because she had something either in her baggage or on her person? She didn't have the profile of a swallower. She was too well dressed, she had too much baggage. She lived here and she answered Wicks's questions with an assurance that wasn't normal with swallowers. Wicksy and a female Officer called Rosie searched her baggage. There was nothing there. Rosie sought, and was granted permission to carry out a full strip search. Mike the SO gave permission for the full strip rather than the less intrusive rub down as there was a possibility she had either swallowed or stuffed packages and a rub down wouldn't help. The full strip wouldn't be a lot of help, but there might just be some tell-tale signs, especially if she'd stuffed the packages.

Miss Hairdo was given her rights and escorted to a Search Box, so called because they were no more than four walls with a chair and a desk. No washing facilities. Very minimalist so nothing could be hidden during the search. No roof so if BAA desired to reconfigure the Green Channel they could do more easily. It was just a box and it was only used for searching people. Hence it was a Search Box. Rosie carried out the search while a second female Officer, Brenda, noted down everything that took place. Rosie was working her way down, she hadn't looked in the mouth or the hair, but she had done everything else except those two areas and the feet. Miss Hairdo had removed her tights and her shoes and Rosie was on her knees looking between her toes and under the soles of her feet. Brenda had her head down writing her note of what Rosie was doing. At this point Miss Hairdo gave a yelp, the two Officers looked up to see her throw something over the top of the Search Box. Miss Hairdo put her face into her hands and started sobbing. There was blood everywhere. Almost immediately Wicksy hammered on the door and let them know that a wig had descended into the Green Channel from the heavens and he had secured it.

As Rosie and Brenda looked at Miss Hairdo they realised what she had done. She had been wearing a very elaborate hairstyle. In fact it was a wig. Miss Hairdo had taken the opportunity when neither Officer was looking directly at her, to whip the wig off and throw it over the top into the Green Channel. If she'd thrown it in the other direction it would have landed in the Red Channel behind the Officers who were working there. In that case it might have gone unnoticed. She either forgot, or in her desperation she ignored the fact that the wig was sewn into her own her hair. When she pulled it off it took whole clumps of her own hair and her scalp with it. Very painful, and all to no avail. When the dust settled and the wig could be looked at properly it was found to contain a kilo of cocaine. By the time Miss Hairdo finally arrived at Isleworth Crown Court her hair was almost fully grown back, but despite this the Judge decided she needed another five and a half years in Holloway for it to completely recover its' former glory.

This type of wig was almost impossible to detect just from looking at it. They were always made of human hair so there was no clue in the texture or the feel of it. It was a favourite concealment of young Jamaican and West African ladies. They tend to have very thick hair so even feeling the top of the head didn't always give it away. Very often officers would have to cut the wig away, using scissors, before they could be sure. This was particularly tricky because it really was impossible to "see the join", and no doubt a few clumps of real hair disappeared over the years. But nobody was really in a position to complain. On one auspicious occasion an Officer; to spare his blushes we'll call him Sebastian because there was no Officer called Sebastien, was half way through removing the "wig" when it became obvious to everyone involved that the wig wasn't actually a wig. It was the lady's real hair. The young lady involved wasn't particularly happy, she had been telling them it wasn't a wig at the top of her voice. Still she had plenty of time for the hair to grow again as she was also about to occupy a bijou cell in Holloway for the next three and a half years. She didn't have anything under her hair but she did have approximately two-hundred packages of cocaine in her stomach.

The other important thing about concealments in wigs, was that they tended to come in batches. No drug organisation worth their salt would bother to go to the trouble of obtaining the human hair, and paying a wigmaker, just to make one wig with a mere half a kilo or even a kilo inside it. No they would have several done at the same time and send over twenty or thirty kilos. Half a kilo or a kilo at a time.

**

Although concealments were becoming more and more difficult to detect, it was important, as has been said before, not to forget the "bleedin' obvious."

Nick, John, and Colin were members of the Terminal Two Baggage Team working under a Senior Officer who we'll call Bill. Baggage Teams didn't have to adhere to a roster which was very nice. However, sometimes they had to work on information until it was dealt with or aborted, and this wasn't quite so nice. On one occasion in the mid-eighties they were passed information that two Brazilian brothers by the name of Bernadi, would be attempting to import a large amount of cocaine on a Swissair flight. They were given a time span of thirty days in which this importation would take place. This meant that they had to cover every Swissair flight that landed in Terminal Two during that time. As the first Swissair flight was very early in the morning and the last one about nine o'clock in the evening this meant that they were in for some very long days. They were hoping desperately that the brothers would turn up sooner rather than later. But no such luck. Day after day, no sign of the Bernadis. The team were split to cover all flights every day. It was a long thirty days. Nick,

Colin, and John were on duty on day thirty. Nothing in the morning, nothing in the afternoon, the very last flight landed at 21.15. The team couldn't believe it, as they were doing their checks in the Immigration Lounge, they had a result, the Bernadis were there.

The lads kept them under observation as they made their way to the Reclaim Hall. There was brief discussion about who would stop who, if they came through individually. One was quite a bit older than the other, so it was felt the younger one was the best bet. John insisted that he would stop the younger Bernadi, Nick not being one to get upset about minutiae, let him have his way. Colin would jockey with Nick. As expected the Bernadis stood apart whilst they were waiting round the reclaim belt.

The younger Bernadi picked up his suitcase and proceeded to make his way to the Green Channel. John intercepted him. Then the elder Bernadi picked up his suitcase and followed his brother in to the Green, where Nick was waiting for him. The team were expecting a reasonable weight of drugs but they weren't prepared for what they found. John searching the younger brother, found nothing. Nick searching the older of the two found approximately twenty two kilos of cocaine in the biggest, deepest and most obvious double bottom concealment that he or anybody else had ever seen. It was about half the depth of the suitcase. John was chagrined, Nick was elated, and everybody was amazed. The suitcase when emptied of clothes, weighed twenty six kilos. It was, and probably still is, a record for amount of cocaine actually concealed in the double bottom of a suitcase. The smugglers might be getting more devious and cleverer, but as was stated previously, it didn't pay to ignore the "bleedin obvious"

**

The concealments were getting more devious and more sophisticated. The officers of HM Customs were always playing catch up. That was the name of the game. They couldn't actually get ahead of the game, because to discover the latest concealment the smuggler had to have thought of it first. The only thing they could do was to make sure that any new methodology was picked up on as soon as possible.

**

Bluff and counter bluff in the Red

Although drug seizures in the Red Channel were less frequent than in the Green, they weren't unknown. Whether to use the Red or Green was a loaded question for the would-be smuggler. If they went through the Green they stood a good chance of not having to speak to an officer at all. However if they were stopped they then had to almost prove their innocence. Whereas if they went into the Red Channel, although they knew they would indeed have to speak to an officer. They were in a position that said "Look at me I'm an honest man or woman, coming to declare my excess goods, surely you can't think I'm a drug smuggler?" Sadly for us, we know this bluff did work. There were many small cannabis seizures off of flights such as the JM001 and the BA262, both from Kingston Jamaica. On these flights the passengers would invariably have excess rum and would come into the Red to declare it. Hoping that the declaration would be accepted, they would pay the duty, and then they would hope to go on their way with their stash of gear tucked away in their suitcase. But there were very few Class A drug seizures.

**

A brand new Officer; let's call him Fred; was on duty in the Red Channel, Terminal Three. This story has been touched on briefly in a previous Chapter but deserves a fuller explanation. It was early morning and all the Far East flights were coming through, so it was pretty busy in the Red. The year was 1982 and places like Hong Kong, Singapore, and Bangkok were still selling goods such as cameras, radios, tape recorders, etc., at prices that meant you could buy them there, pay the duty and still be quids in. So early in the morning when there were flights from all places East of Teheran touching down, the Red tended to be very busy.

Fred had only just finished his training course and he was still very wet behind the ears, so he was taking things very steadily. Assessing duty on electrical items, making sure people weren't overcharged, could be very complicated. On top of that making sure that although they appeared to be honest, they were actually declaring the full value, or indeed were declaring everything they had obtained, could be tricky. It wasn't easy showing that you didn't entirely trust someone who was an ostensibly honest person. It was a very delicate procedure. The passenger was, as stated, apparently honest. But by the very fact that the Officer was questioning the passenger further, asking for further proof; not just a receipt; searching baggage, he or she was showing that they didn't entirely believe the passengers declaration. So the Red Channel could be a minefield, especially to a new recruit.

Fred's relief when Mr Sim appeared before him and declared a single bottle of Johnny Walker Red Label Whisky in excess of his allowance, was considerable. No problem here, easy to calculate the duty on a bottle of Whisky, Mr Sim is a visitor here, a business man so he is unlikely to have the type of goods a returning resident might have. He comes here more or less every three months, he always brings a bottle of Red Label for his business partner because Red Label isn't available in the UK at present. So it's nice and easy, he knows he's got some money to pay. He looks smart, he travelled Business Class; Fred can see the tag on his suitcase; he's very articulate and speaks perfect English. This is almost like a training exercise for Fred.

Now Fred isn't actually thinking about searching any of the baggage, but at this point Mr Sim can't find his wallet so he puts his briefcase on the bench and opens it to see if it's in there. Mr Sim opens the briefcase and finds his wallet, he takes out a £10 note and hands it to Fred. At this point, and he was never able to explain why. It was probably to kill time dealing with a nice easy declaration. You never know the next one might be something a bit more complicated. Fred decides to look in the briefcase. It's open, it's there in front of him he's not doubting Mr Sim's honesty, for whatever reason, he just decides to look in it.

"I'll just have a quick look in the briefcase as it's open, if you don't mind," says Fred. Very polite was young Fred

As a matter of fact Mr Sim definitely does mind but he can't really say anything. And why does Mr Sim not want Fred looking into his briefcase. Because inside the briefcase, in a very obvious double lining, are concealed five kilos of heroin. That's why.

Fred immediately involves his colleague in the Red Channel and Mr Sim is escorted into the box. It transpired that Mr Sim has being coming to this country four times a year for the last five years. From what he had said in the Red he had declared bottles of whisky on previous occasions. If he had five kilos of smack on every trip that's one-hundred kilos of 75% pure heroin he has smuggled in. Of course, it was the first time he'd tried it! He admitted to this offence. He couldn't very well deny it, as it was such a clumsy concealment. But it was definitely the first time. It was strange though, if as he claimed it really was the first and only time, what had he been coming here for. The business partner and his address did not check out. Although the business and his address did check out in Singapore. He had plenty of business documents for importing and exporting a variety of goods. He had no hotel booking or address to stay at. He mentioned places he was going to buy goods but he had no appointments or meetings. His cash paid ticket showed that he would only be here for 3 nights. So where was he going to stay. He repeatedly 'no replied' to these and other questions.

Eventually it was decided to just charge him with the attempted fraudulent evasion of the prohibition in respect of the five kilos. This would almost certainly mean he would spend upwards of eight years in one of Her Majesty's more basic establishments.

If nothing else this seizure demonstrated that the Red Channel was a risk, and that appearing as an honest traveller making a simple declaration did have many advantages over running the gauntlet in the Green.

**

Paul M, a pleasant easy going Officer was working in the Red Channel, Terminal Three, and the Iran Air was coming through. It was 1979 and drug smugglers were becoming more sophisticated. But at this time Customs Officers were still paid rewards on goods they seized so Paul was thinking as much about revenue goods as he was about drugs. He was a conscientious Officer who took his time, and dealt with everyone the same calm way. A Mr Akbari presented a fine silk carpet for examination. He was declaring it because it had cost one-hundred and fifty pounds and it was in excess of his twenty-eight pound allowance and he wanted to pay the duty on the excess. It was a lovely carpet with very intricate patterns and high density of knots per square inch. This is what determines the value of carpets. The higher the density of knots and hence the closeness of the weave is the main determining factor when looking at the value. The density of knots on this carpet was extremely high.

Paul not only wasn't happy with the valuation he wasn't happy with the man. Something wasn't right. Akbari had produced a receipt showing US Dollars that equated to one-hundred and fifty UK pounds. This was meaningless. Duplicate receipts with one showing the real value, for insurance purposes, and one showing a reduced value for Customs, were only too common. These were the days of the Peacock Throne in Iran and the Shah was still sitting on it. The country was as capitalist as the USA and Europe, and drugs were freely available. There was heroin from Afghanistan and the Golden Triangle, and there was cannabis from everywhere east of the Lebanon.

Paul wasn't happy with the valuation so he had a quick look in the Green to see if there was anybody who would have more information. He spotted his mate Paul D. Now Paul was a top level Officer in both drugs and revenue offence situations. He came into the Red and spoke to Mr Akbari. Mr Akbari insisted the carpet was only worth one-hundred and fifty pounds. Paul D wasn't happy. Mr Akbari was making a big, big mistake. He was, it turned out, trying to defraud Customs at the same time as he was trying to import heroin. This is not a good idea. Paul D was turning the carpet over and over. And as he was doing it he was noticing something not quite right with the texture. It felt ever so slightly tacky or sticky. It wasn't as smooth as silk should be. It was as if it had had something spilt on it. Mr Akbari was now getting extremely agitated and was demanding to know what all the fuss was about. He'd shown the receipt so what was the problem?

The two Pauls knew something wasn't right and Paul D was becoming more and more sure it wasn't just an under declaration of the value.

Geoff the SO appeared, wanting to know what all the fuss was about. Paul M explained about the disputed value of the carpet and Paul D added his bit about the texture of the carpet. Geoff had a look at the carpet and he also wasn't happy. So now there were three unhappy Customs officials and an extremely unhappy passenger. Eventually Geoff suggested a field test to see if it gave a positive reaction to heroin. The problem that the two Pauls had was that the field test for heroin is to drop a small grain of powder into a small glass phial containing a chemical reagent. So how to get enough of the suspect textile into the phial? They tried dropping very small pieces of the carpet pile into a phial but the dye on the pile was confusing the reaction. The Officers were looking for a purple to red reaction. Sometimes it would be such a deep purple that it would appear to be almost black. But their problem was that they couldn't tell if it was a heroin reaction or if it was the dye. Finally they took piece of filter paper rubbed it on the carpet and dropped a tiny piece into the phial. It turned a lovely purple colour. Between them the two Pauls had found the first seizure of fabric, in this case, a carpet, saturated with a heroin solution. The carpet was sent to the Government Chemist and over two kilos of 80% pure smack was retrieved. Mr Akbari denied everything. It was a no reply interview. At the time when he was cautioned he was warned that it was, "you're right to remain silent but that anything he said would be taken down and might be given in evidence." This later changed and suspects were cautioned that, "It may harm your defence if you fail to mention something that you later rely on in court". Because of this at the time of Mr Akbaris's arrest Customs Officers were often met with "No reply". Sometimes it would be in reply to a particularly pertinent question and sometimes it would carry on throughout the whole interview. The sad thing was that the Judge would always advise the members of the jury that couldn't assume anything just because someone had declined to answer a question.

So you would have the following scenario;

Q: How long are you coming here for?

A: Three weeks.

Q: Why are you coming here?

A: See/visit some relatives.

Q: Do you agree you told me that this is your suitcase?

A: Yes.

Q: And do you agree that you told me that you were aware of the contents of the suitcase?

A: Yes I did.

Q: And you told me that weren't carrying any packages or parcels For anyone else.

A: No reply.

Q;   And you were present when I opened and searched your suitcase?

A: Yes that is correct.

Q: Do you recognise this package?
       (Indicating a brown package sealed with brown tape).

A: No reply.

Q: Do you agree that it came out of your suitcase?

A: No reply.

At which point the judge warns the jury not to read anything into the "no reply" responses.

Eventually when tape recorded interviews came into being, Officers would become expert at asking the questions in such a way that it became obvious to the Jury why the defendant was not answering the more pertinent ones. However the Officers still needed to be very careful. Ask a no reply question too many times and it wasn't unknown for the Judge to rule part of or the whole tape recording inadmissible or prejudicial.

Anyway, the jury in the case of Customs versus Akbari obviously did read something into the no replies, because they found him guilty and he was sentenced to four and a half years in the 'Scrubs'. Akbari was a fool and he was greedy. He had a superb concealment which hadn't been seen before. The carpet was worth six-hundred pounds; Paul M found the real receipt when he strip searched him. The duty and tax would have been approximately one-hundred and fifty pounds, the heroin was worth about one-hundred thousand pounds on the streets. So to save one-hundred and fifty; what he would have paid in duty on the real value; he not only lost one-hundred thousand pounds, he also ended up inside.

Heroin solution wasn't only found in carpets, very often it was in heavy items of clothing. The methodology was quite complicated. The would-be smuggler prepares a solution that includes the heroin. The item is then soaked in the solution and allowed to dry. Now this is the tricky bit. If they don't let it dry enough then whatever the textile is it will feel a bit tacky or sticky. Which is what Paul D could feel. However if they dry it too much it will go powdery and if you gently rub it you can actually see the heroin dust. When they reach their destination, after they've successfully negotiated Customs, they just do the reverse. They soak the garment or carpet in water. They then allow it to drain into a metal tub and simmer the liquid until all that is left is the heroin. This type of concealment is almost impossible to detect if it is done properly, and the only reason it is not more widely used, in fact it appears not to be used at all now, is that there is some loss of heroin in the process. And of course heroin is just too valuable to waste.

**

A young IC1 British male by the name of Bridge from Greater Manchester summed up the cunning and at the same time the stupidity that was at times displayed by the would be smuggler.

Rob, or HT as he was known by his mates in Terminal Four, was having a quiet day in the Red Channel. He hadn't been in uniform that long but he was doing alright. A smashing bloke, well-liked by all his colleagues, he appreciated good food, good wine, a nice cigar, and cricket. In fact on this particular day he was looking forward to an evening with friends during which the first three of those things he appreciated would be on the agenda. The cricket was another matter. He personally was having a rather lean time and the England cricket team was in its' usual state of turmoil. He was 'Mr laid-back'. He finished with one passenger and looked up to see who was next in the queue. Lo and behold there was Mr Bridge. On his trolley there was a suitcase, a briefcase, and the biggest ghetto blaster HT had ever seen.

HT went through the usual questions. Mr Bridge had been to the Far East on business. Tokyo, Hong Kong, Singapore, Bangkok, and home. He was relaxed, seemed natural, asked how England were doing in the cricket. This wasn't a good question as England had just been thrashed by India. One of those rare Tests when Gooch didn't reach double figures in either innings. Anyway it all appeared quite natural and easy, and his business credentials stood up to scrutiny.

Mr Bridge was declaring the ghetto blaster which he'd bought two days previously in Bangkok. It did seem a bit cheap. Bridge explained that he'd only bought it to use while he was away and it only ran on batteries so this made it cheaper because of the cost of having to keep buying batteries. This didn't quite add up either. If it was only to use while he was away, why did he buy it two days before he came home? But people do funny things. As a Customs Officer you soon become aware that there is no such thing as "normal behaviour". HT isn't particularly suspicious, the blaster is only one-hundred and fifty pounds, so if it is an under declaration, it's not going to be a big deal. But he asks to see the receipt just in case.

The young Mancunian stood before him opens his briefcase to find the receipt. HT immediately notices eight D size batteries. Presumably the ones from the blaster.

"They didn't last long," says HT.

"Oh no they're still working," says Bridge.

Now, as I've already said, HT is a laid back sort of guy, but he is now feverishly thinking. If the batteries are still working, why take them out of the ghetto blaster? It's not as if he's packed them in his suitcase to make it lighter to carry. They're in the briefcase, so he's still physically carrying them. Some people remove batteries in case they leak. But this can't be the reason if it's only two days old. Doesn't make sense. He looks up at Bridge and Bridges' demeanour has done a 360 degree turn. From

Mr Ever-So-Calm, he now looks like the proverbial rabbit staring into the headlights. A second Officer has appeared as if by magic.

"Need a hand TH," he asks?

This rather strange Officer calls him TH rather than the usual HT. Nobody knows why and nobody really cares. The blaster is still on the trolley and is out of reach for HT.

"You couldn't flip the lid of the battery compartment for me?" asks HT?

Grant, the rather strange Officer, obliges. Guess what, the battery compartment is full of a small amount of heroin and what turns out to be a liquid form of amphetamine. This is very unusual. Amphetamine is normally a categorised as Class B but when it is in a form that can be injected it is reclassified as Class A. Mr Bridge is trying to look surprised, but he's not doing it very well. Eventually he admits attempted evasion of the prohibition. He was a regular traveller, and for whatever reason, maybe he decided confession is good for the soul, he admitted to four previous runs.

Bridge certainly wasn't the fizziest drink in the fridge. But he was typical of a type of semi-professional smuggler who thought they could buck the system, and on this occasion failed. He had a good job, but would it be waiting for him after three years in Strangeways? He was one of that small band of drug smugglers who actually have a legitimate reason for travel. Sadly for him he was just too stupid to make the most of it.

**

Now you might be wondering how anybody could be that stupid. Luckily for us some smugglers would have set up a really smart and sophisticated system and then let themselves down by doing something ridiculous. Now this next story has nothing to do with the Red Channel but it does illustrate just how daft they can be.

A young officer who we will call DC was on a six to two shift. DC was an easy going likeable officer. Sort of bloke who everybody seemed to know. Normally for good reasons. It was June July time, DC was on a Rummage Crew working on the Tarmac. The Tarmac was good in the summer, unless it was raining of course. The Senior Officer had decided to cover the bags on the American Airways AA56. This flight was a good connector. It started life in Buenos Aires, transited Miami, then after Heathrow it went on to Amsterdam. So as you can see there were drug connections all along the line. The drugs could start in BA and be targeted for London or Amsterdam. Or they could be put on in Miami and again be aimed at either London or Amsterdam. On one remarkable occasion they were put on in BA supposedly going to Miami, but ended up at LHR. The whole flight was full of potential, but of course heading for Amsterdam the transit bags were the best bet. DC was working with two Officers who will call Marty and JC. There were others around, another Bob and a Den. So there was bags, excuse the pun, of experience. DC loved working in a team and was therefore a very good team member. This situation was just what DC liked. Work with every chance of a positive result, surrounded by colleagues, in the fresh air, well to be more accurate fresh diesel fumes, loads of good humoured sarcastic banter. Brilliant. But then for DC it got a whole lot better.

He had selected an America Tourister. He liked this particular type of suitcase, as it had a natural void round the base and the sides. He opened the suitcase, there being an airline representative there of course! He used his master key and worked out the combination, a skill most officers acquired very quickly. It's one of those things once learnt you never forget. Quite useful at times. A quick look in the suitcase indicated there was nothing in the cavities, but lo and behold there were parcels all wrapped up in Christmas paper. Now this is July, DC wonders why someone is carrying Christmas presents around in the middle of summer, more than five months before Christmas. The packages all contained cans of shaving foam. Strange sort of present thinks DC. Would anyone have six friends who would appreciate a can of shaving foam? Now DC is pretty sharp but you really don't need to be Sherlock Holmes to realise something isn't quite right.

DC could see there had been soldering carried out on the bottom of the cans. But there was some debate whether or not to cut them open. Probably not a good idea if they had been tampered with. Nobody wants to end up covered in foam and ruining the evidence. However BAA had recently installed a brand new x-ray machine airside, so DC and his boss JC, no religious connection, trotted along and x-rayed them. It was a clever concealment. They had opened the can put in the coke, then a small foam dispenser had been placed in such a position that if you squeezed the nozzle foam would come out. You could even hear the foam slushing about when you shook them. Very clever. Shame about the Christmas paper.

All they needed to do now was find the perpetrator. They had the name, McLoud, and they knew he was in transit. So along with the Investigation Team they went to the Transit Lounge. McLoud, an Argentinian national, was very smartly dressed, and looked like a genuine business man. Under different circumstances you wouldn't have looked at him twice. He spoke good English and the whole thing soon unravelled. McLoud even boasted that he did a couple of trips a year doing the same thing for upmarket clients who paid him a lot of money.

Except for a rather bizarre little incident between JC and McLoud this would have been the end of a very nice simple little job. Now JC was very conscientious, if a little cautious. As it was late on the Friday before McLoud was charged he had to be held in the Custody Suite over the weekend ready to appear at Uxbridge Magistrates Court on the Monday. This meant the team had to look after him. Not normally a problem and all went well until the Sunday morning. JC is clucking around like a mother hen, trying to get McLoud to have some breakfast. But McLoud doesn't want any breakfast. He just wants to be left alone to get some kip. JC's not having it. He offers tea, coffee, and orange. All politely declined. He gets half way through offering cornfl.... When McLoud loses it and tells JC just what he can do with his f....ing cornflakes. JC, still very calm, explains that it is his responsibility to make sure he is well looked after. "In that case", says McLoud, I want to go to church, I want to repent my sins." JC insisted this request was presented to the Custody Officer who we will call Pat. Pat's reply was unprintable, she didn't suffer fools gladly, but needless to say McLoud did not get the opportunity to repent his sins. Eventually he would end up in Isleworth and would go down for ten years, and DC would end up with a Commendation from the judge.

If only he'd bought some different wrapping paper he might have got away with it. Silly man!

**

It was the 12th of March 1985 and Prem, an Asian Officer, was operating in the Red Channel in Terminal Two. He wasn't a happy bunny. It was his wedding anniversary, but that had nothing to do with his bad mood. His problem was the Duty Senior Officer, affectionately known as "Jet" by the officers. More specifically, his problem was that he was training two new entrants and Jet was interfering. It was practical training and Prem should have been free to deploy himself and his two trainees wherever he thought they would gain most experience. But Jet had decided he needed Prem to supplement his resources in the Red Channel. Jack, the Training and Development Officer would have blown a gasket if he'd known. What made it worse was that two of the three Officers operating in the Red disappeared for breakfast as soon as Prem appeared. Surely they could have been instructed to stagger their breaks. He was told by Jet that it was to enable him to move one of the other Officers who was under performing, into the Green. This didn't make Prem any happier, in his eyes his trainees were suffering to help Jet solve a management issue.

Anyway there he was working in the Red alongside Brian, the third member of the early team. As he was dealing with one passenger he noticed an Asian man approach one of the Terminal Enforcement team, we'll call him Dick, and Dick pointed him in the direction of the Red. He had an extra bottle of whisky and he needed to declare it.

Prem asked the usual questions and established that he was dealing with a Mr Tarlochan Singh Aujlay, known as Torchie to his friends. He was resident in the UK and was on his way back from Delhi via Amsterdam and he had a bottle of Grants whisky to declare. Nothing unusual so far. Prem kept looking at his hard sided suitcase which interested him. He was thinking that a false top and bottom or sides could hold up to ten kilos of smack. He then asked Torchie if he had anything else to declare. Now whether or not Prem had spooked him by his frequent glances at his suitcase we will never know, but at this point Torchie did a strange thing. He declared a Citizen wristwatch that he was wearing. It was obviously a used watch. He then went on to explain that he had bought it in Amsterdam City Centre. Now Prem knew this was a lie. He could see the transit tags on his suitcase. Torchie hadn't actually entered Holland, he hadn't left Amsterdam Airport. So why had he lied? Was he just trying to divert attention away from his suitcase? Prem asked to look into his briefcase. It was a style of briefcase much beloved by aircrew and Torchie then explained that he was deadheading crew. That is, he was crew who had worked on the outward flight, but hadn't worked on the return trip. He was a British Airways Steward. This increased Prems concerns. Air crew knew the ropes, they knew where the cheapest places in the world were to buy things. They also travelled very frequently for genuine reasons so they could be used to carry parcels and packages without raising undue suspicion. It was simple as they didn't need to make up a pack of lies to justify their journey. Unlike most mules, who had no good reason to travel, so they had to lie about what they were doing.

As Prem looked through the briefcase he noticed that Torchie was sweating profusely and was dabbing his forehead with his handkerchief. This was strange because it wasn't hot. It was March and the central heating in the old Terminal Two was never very efficient. He decided to have a look inside the Echolac suitcase.

Prem, who was always polite, asked to look in the first suitcase. He didn't have to ask, it was his right to look. But he was always polite. "Torchies" reply was less polite.

"Yes, keep the f***ing thing I'm off to Rio in the morning". Right out of the blue, completely unprovoked. It was most strange. But it was also very typical of a certain type of person who was up to something. They would suddenly adopt a confrontational stance and become quite aggressive. Almost as if the best form of defence was attack.

This sudden outburst convinced Prem that there was something in the suitcase. Sure enough, in amongst his clothes he found two packages, approximately 10" x 4", sewn up with denim. He could smell a familiar smell even through the denim. He knew immediately that he was dealing with heroin.

"What's this?" He asked Torchie.

Prem was then told that Torchie had been asked by an old friend of his fathers to bring back some Indian sugar and deliver it to him in Southall. He explained that this type of sugar wasn't available in the UK. Unusual. But not unheard of.

"But I asked you if you were carrying any packages for anyone", said Prem.

"I didn't think you'd be interested in a couple of bags of sugar." Came the prompt reply.

"But I actually asked you twice. But you still didn't mention them."

Torchie shrugged, "Just didn't cross my mind."

Brian, working alongside Prem, knew what was going on. He slipped away and let the Enforcement Team know what was occurring in the Red. The SO, we'll call him Pete, because that was his name, was not amused when he heard that this potential heroin seizure had been waived away by one of his team. But linking with the local Investigation Unit, he arranged a "run" while Prem was completing his examination in the Red.

The Officer clarified with Torchie that the packages contained sugar, and returned them into the suitcase. He now controlled the adrenalin rush that had almost consumed him, kept himself together, and professional to the last, took the money on the extra bottle. He admitted privately afterwards that in his excitement he overcharged him. But Torchie, who as a BA Steward would have known the proper charge down to the last penny, didn't say a word. He obviously had more important things on his mind.

Incredibly the run was successful. I say incredible because Prem felt Torchie must have known that he was on to him. They didn't have to follow him far to make the connection with the next link in the chain. Torchie wheeled his trolley down the ramp and outside Terminal Two Departures he met up with a man driving his own mini cab. This was good news. The cab driver was local. He lived just off of the Uxbridge Road in Hayes. His house was searched and evidence was found showing that he was using his cab business as a front for the importation and trafficking of heroin. But he wasn't a complete idiot. Although it was obvious what was going on, no names of other couriers or contacts for selling were found. Despite not being able to locate the others involved it was still a very nice job.

So why did Torchie, a man with a decent well paid job get involved with drug smuggling? It transpired that Torchie was living way above his means. He was running a Porsche, he was a gambler and a womaniser, and we all know women are expensive. He was eleven thousand pounds in debt. This was a lot of money back in those days. He was charged with the attempted evasion of the prohibition in respect of 9.1 kilos of heroin, and at Reading Crown Court he was duly found guilty and sentenced to nine years at HMP.

The bluff of declaring an extra bottle might have worked, but Torchie just ran into the wrong Officer. Or I suppose the right Officer if you look at it from the opposite perspective.

**

Torchie was obviously an amateur. Not a professional mule. If he had been he would have been much more wary when approaching his contact. Strange, odd, bizarre things often happened when amateurs became involved in drug smuggling. Chris, who we have already met in this book, and Mike, were standing in the DSO's office when the phone rang and it was BAA Security at one of the many Departure Gates in Terminal Three. Somebody had discarded a jacket and it felt a bit heavy.

When they reached the Departure Gate the BAA Security Guard handed over a very heavy lumber style jacket in a plastic tray. It had been left on a chair. As the Officers carefully lifted it by the coat hook it was obvious there was something hidden in the pocket linings. The Security Guard didn't know who it belonged to. There had been a hell of a rush, people being rubbed down, people running to catch planes. A little bit of mayhem. Then when it quietened down, there was the jacket sitting in the tray that it had gone through the x-ray on. They'd put it back through the x-ray just in case there were explosives in it, but it was clear. They could see a couple of large brown blobs that didn't make sense. Now this was good work by the Security Guards. They were given some familiarisation and recognition training by Customs Officers like Mike and Reg who we heard of earlier, but on the x-ray the drugs would have been the same colour as the jacket. Any drug that was derived from something that started life as a plant would show up as brown. The jacket would have been made from something that started life as a plant, so this would show up as brown. Even if it was mixed with synthetic substances the drug would look the same as any other item that was originally plant life. So this was a good spot by the guards and it was even better that they had the sense to know not to touch it. On examination the Officers found a quantity of cocaine in the linings.

The nearest flight to the CP was the Varig which had come in from Rio de Janeiro via Lisbon and was on its' way to New York. Chris and Mike stopped the departure of the flight and boarded the plane. Chris walked up and down the aisle carrying the jacket and eventually confronted a middle aged South American looking man. Why him? Well for one thing he wasn't wearing a jacket, but mainly it was because he just appeared extremely nervous, worried, and uncomfortable.

Amazingly the man admitted it was his. There was no way Chris could have proved it was his if he hadn't. There was nothing personal in the pockets, no name tag. If he had kept quiet HM Customs couldn't have touched him. He was escorted from the aircraft and when his person was searched he was found to have cocaine strapped round his legs. Altogether he had over four kilos of cocaine.

What was never explained was why he suddenly lost his nerve. He had travelled all the way from Rio, presumably with some of it strapped to his legs. Then when it lands at LHR instead of just sitting tight and staying on the plane he decides to get off and have a wander around Terminal Three. He doesn't land himself so he doesn't go through Customs controls He then makes his way back to the flight and then after all this time carrying the drugs, he panics.

But why oh why had he ditched the jacket; or did he take it off and forget it, not very likely; and then having ditched it why did he admit it was his. Quite simply he was a University Professor trying to raise funds for a political cause back in South America. He probably ditched the jacket because he thought the Security Guards were Customs Officers. Many passengers are under that misapprehension. And then on the aircraft, the fact that Chris approached him, probably convinced him that Chris knew it was his. So he thought the game was up.

In short, he was an amateur, and amateurs do silly things. Thank goodness.

**

Letting it run

Although it was very satisfying to catch a courier with drugs, and make no mistake about it this is a good result, the aim if possible was always to let the mule run and see where he, or she, led us. Sometimes this would be done with the mule's assistance. They would hope that it might reduce the sentence. But most times it would be done without their knowledge. If it was to be done without their knowledge, which was obviously preferable because it removed the possibility that they might tip off whoever was due to be meeting them, the Officer had to find the drugs without chummy knowing that he was on to him. Sometimes this would be quite easy; a double sided suitcase could be detected just by moving it about on the bench whilst you were inspecting it. The especially stiff sides and the extra weight are easy to detect. The next problem for the Officer is to alert his colleagues without alerting the client. This could be done by picking on a quite innocent object and telling the smuggler that you are going to test it for drugs, or maybe by pretending that the Officer thought there was something suspicious about the passport and asking a colleague to check it out. The beauty about both of these ruses was that the suspect would be quite happy that there was nothing to be found. The Officer then disappears and alerts his Senior Officer who informs the Investigation boys who organise a run. In later years, Alpha One the Duty Surveyor would take responsibility for initiating runs. But the run itself would be carried out and controlled by the Investigators, the people in plain clothes. The Officer then returns to the bench and tells the client that the item has tested negative, or that the Passport is genuine, or whatever he said he was going to check. He then detains chummy as long as he can without raising his suspicions and lets him go. By this time Officers in civvies are waiting outside to follow him. Some teams adopted more sophisticated ways of alerting their colleagues. For example one team would find a reason to ask a colleague to go and get something for them. The conversation would go something like this:

Officer A: "Can you go and get me a spare notebook I've left mine in my pigeon hole in Building 820?"

Now officer B knows that Officer A doesn't need a spare notebook. Indeed he knows that he can't have a spare notebook. All notebooks are uniquely numbered and are only issued when a notebook is exhausted and needs replacing. This makes the auditing a lot more simple and it cuts out a lot of silly Defence questions in Court about when exactly was the notebook written. However Officer B knows that this is the team code for "I think I've got a commercial quantity. Go and see if Alpha One wants to run it." Officer B then says to Officer A:

"Sorry mate, I haven't got a spare do you want me to go and see if Alpha One's got one?"

He knows Alpha One hasn't got a spare. Nobody can have a spare notebook. But this is Officer B's way of making sure Officer A wants a run organised.

"Yes if you don't mind," says Officer A.

Officer B trots off and informs Alpha One, or in earlier days the Duty Senior Officer, or his own Team Leader.

Whoever the person in charge is makes the decision and informs Officer B that he or she needs 15 or 20 minutes to get the plain clothes people into position. Officer B would then return to the Green Channel and would give Officer A something that looked like a notebook. This would be the sign that the run was on. If the run wasn't on then Officer B would have returned empty handed.

If the run was on as Officer B handed over the dummy notebook he would add almost as an afterthought:

"How much longer are you going to be with him only we're all off to breakfast in 15 minutes?"

Officer A now knows that he needs to keep the suspect in the Green Channel for a further 15 minutes.

"How do I know how long I'll be, how long's a piece of string?"

He will keep the mule for 15 minutes by very slowly looking in every imaginable place in the baggage where he knows there aren't any drugs. Doesn't always work of course, one Officer feverishly beavering away, trying to kill time, unrolled a tube of toothpaste and much to his horror found two bits of cannabis resin tucked away in the bottom.

In the early years the run was very unprofessional but fortunately for us so were a lot of the smugglers. The case of "Torchie" in the previous Chapter exemplifies this. Despite all the shenanigans in the Red and Prems' obvious suspicions, Torchie still thought he had pulled it off.

**

In 1977 we weren't sophisticated enough to use codes but Customs were still able to follow suspects without their knowledge. Maybe the smugglers weren't as switched on as we thought they were.

Chak, who you will hear more of later, was stood in the Green Channel in Terminal Two. He was on a seven to three shift so he wasn't particularly happy. Chak didn't like earlies he preferred to be late, and in reality he usually was. Late that is. He wasn't an early bird, and he always felt that someone else could have the worm as long as he could have the flights that arrived after lunch in Terminal Two. Most of the good connectors, that is a flight that arrives from a low risk airport, normally European, but which has passengers on board who have transited from a high risk flight, landed after lunch, and these connectors were a constant source of high quality Class A drug detections. Flying from somewhere like Lagos and going to Brussels then catching an onward flight to Heathrow was a ploy often used by the organisations trying to import commercial quantities of drugs.

However back to Chak. It was a Sunday, which did cheer him up a little as it meant he was on double time, which was nice. A KLM flight from

Amsterdam was in the Hall and its passengers were filtering through. Chak noticed a young black passenger in a white safari suit talking to another Officer at the mouth of the Green Channel. He was carrying a Suit Carrier and a bright yellow Amsterdam Duty Free Shop carrier bag. The Officer the young man was speaking to wasn't interested, but Chak certainly was. There had been a spate of seizures recently in which the offender had fitted the profile of the young black passenger.

Chak duly intercepted him. He quickly established that his name was Honest Obasanjo Kaye. He was a resident of Nigeria, and he was travelling on business. He had arrived in the UK thirteen days previously and he had spent nine days here before going to Amsterdam for four days. He was now here to meet with a UK supplier of Land Rover gear box parts. It all seemed in order. The stamps in his passport showed that he had indeed arrived here thirteen days previously and had then travelled to Amsterdam nine days later. He was carrying excess cigarettes. He had two cartons of three-hundred John Players Special cigarettes and he had a litre of spirits. Chak was satisfied. Nine times out of ten it was the ridiculous reason for travel that gave the-would be smuggler away. But Kaye's story held up and appeared entirely plausible. There was documentation to confirm what he was staying and there are many genuine motor traders who travel between Nigeria and Europe buying spare parts for the better makes of car. He did have a cash paid ticket which as has been said several times already, was often an indication of someone who didn't want to leave an audit trail. Someone like a drug smuggler. However if he had bought the ticket in Nigeria where credit card fraud was prevalent this could explain it. Everything else appeared to be in order.

Chak assessed the revenue. He took the money into the Red Channel and returned to the Green and gave Kaye his receipt. He then let him go. But something was niggling at him. He was sure he hadn't missed anything in the soft sided Suit Carrier. He was pretty sure he wasn't a swallower. He didn't fit the profile and we just didn't get swallowers from Amsterdam. Swallowers mostly, but not always, flew direct to minimise the amount of time the packages were inside them.

Chak watched him all the way down the Green as far as the main door. Something wasn't right. Then it clicked, the bright yellow Amsterdam DFS carrier bag, wasn't as bright yellow as it should have been. In fact it was distinctly dusty and bit crumpled. This didn't make sense as according to Kaye he had only just bought the cigarettes a couple of hours ago.

Chak called him back.

"Where did you say you bought your Duty Free cigarettes?" Chak asked.

Kaye smiled and suggested Chak wasn't very good at reading English.

"I bought them in the Amsterdam Duty Free Shop. Can't you read?"

"So where did you store the bag on the aircraft?"

"In the overhead locker".

"So in that case how did it get so dirty and crumpled?"

"How do I know?" Was the terse reply.

Kaye was good, in fact he was very good, and he was acting just as you would expect a disgruntled passenger to act. His attitude could be summed up as someone who had answered all the questions, paid the money and has been allowed to go, but then has been called back for no apparent good reason. Chak checked his passport again. The Immigration stamps were all in order. Chak looked at the cigarettes again. He was now a little suspicious of the weight of the two cartons. Also the bar codes were dirty and unclear. However he pretended he was satisfied. While he was re-examining the suit carrier Chak had managed to alert the Enforcement Team SO, we'll call him Pete. The same Pete that we had met with Torchie. Pete had hastily organised a run, he wanted to know where this young man would lead them. Were there other couriers, was he going to meet the organiser, were they going to unravel something a lot bigger than a single mule?

Kaye was allowed to proceed and obviously thought he had got away with it a second time. This was amazing, he had been stopped, called back, and questioned about the very item that contained the drugs, yet he still thought he was in the clear. Chak had alerted Pete using a nod and a wink, not very subtle, but Torchie still thought he had pulled it off. However he was in a hurry, he had been delayed and he was late. He headed straight for the Underground. The followers kept a discreet distance. It didn't look like Kaye was aware he was being followed, but other people might be watching him, and if we got too close they might realise that he was rumbled.

The officers following; who included Pete the SO, Ron from the local Investigation Unit, and the Joe we meet previously in the interview with Catherine Madeke and the plantains, kept their distance. Kaye showed no hesitation, he marched purposely forward as he obviously thought he was in the clear. The officers who were following were still concerned that they might be being watched by the meeter or meeters. Then they relaxed. Ahead of them they could see who Kaye was hurrying to meet up with. Standing by the Ticket Office was an Afro- Caribbean gentleman – it was later established that he was also Nigerian, though this obviously couldn't be established from a distance - but amazingly he was wearing a white suit, carrying a soft sided suit carrier, and a bright yellow Amsterdam Duty Free Shop carrier bag. Bingo.

As the two of them shook hands and presumably congratulated themselves on their success, Pete, Ron, and the rest of the team moved in and arrested them. Pete had decided that this was the end of the trail. He and Ron thought they were probably the organisers, and the smugglers, and he knew they were heading for the Underground. He wasn't prepared to risk them disappearing into that particular danger area. The chances of picking up their contact over here were slight and it wasn't worth the risk. Kaye and Nwandu had been incredibly amateurish so far, but how long could this go on?

They were returned to Terminal Two. Nwandu, the second Nigerian, also had two three-hundred cigarette cartons, although his were Cartier King

Size cigarettes whereas Kaye had JPS. His DFS bag was also dusty and crumpled. The cigarette cartons, which were commercially intact, were opened and inside were the cigarette packets. Not containing cigarettes, but now full of heroin and cannabis resin. There was a total of 2.5 kilos of the infamous Paki Black cannabis resin, and 1.5 kilos of heroin. Depending on the purity and the street value at the time this payload would be worth over one million pounds on the open market.

The question was how had this happened, and why were the DFS bags so dirty and crumpled? Gradually the story unravelled. Two more passports were found in Nwandu's baggage, these showed stamps in and out of Karachi. There were also two tickets showing they had flown to Pakistan and back during the four days they were supposedly in Amsterdam. Further investigations established that while they were in Karachi they had met up with a gentleman by the name of Massood. He had a contact in a cigarette factory. The cartons of cigarettes which they had bought in Amsterdam, were unwrapped. The cigarettes were removed and replaced with the resin and heroin. The packets were returned to the cartons and the cartons were taken to the factory and put through the packaging machine. And "voila", there we have it. Four commercially intact cartons of cigarettes. They're clever and devious these smugglers. But on this occasion not clever and devious enough. Chak could never understand why they still had the backup passports and the tickets to Karachi. Perhaps the tickets were tax deductible.

Kaye and Nwandu duly appeared at Uxbridge Magistrates Court and amazingly were granted bail. This was amazing. They were both Nigerian nationals with no firm ties in this country, they had demonstrated that they knew how to obtain false passports, yet they were granted bail. Nwandu, obviously not a man to look a gift horse in the mouth, took full advantage of his unexpected freedom and fled straight back home to Nigeria. Kaye, for whatever reason decided to stay, and was found guilty at Isleworth Crown Court and sentenced to five years.

That's the end of that, thought Chak. Almost, but not quite. Some years later Chak received a call from a certain Chief Superintendent from New Scotland Yard.

"Do you know of a Nigerian by the name of Valentino Chukwuka Nwandu?" The Chief Superintendent asked.

"Do I?" Said Chak.

After Nwandu had fled to Nigeria he had returned to his old ways. He obviously hadn't improved very much because four years later he was being held by Danish Customs for trying to import five kilos of heroin from Karachi. Chak travelled to Copenhagen to identify Nwandu. Nwandu got eight years for his Danish escapade. With the information we received from the Copenhagen Customs we established that Nwandu had a flat in Crawley with a Mercedes in the garage. Thanks to a soft hearted Magistrate at Uxbridge, which was strange as most of them were far from soft hearted, Nwandu had an extra four years to ply his trade in and out of European cities. He was never extradited to face the outstanding charges in the UK.

The "run" had succeeded. Chak could have simply arrested Kaye and been happy with a mule and the drugs he was carrying. But no, he wasn't satisfied and as a result Nwandu, probably the driving force behind it all, was also apprehended.

**

Chris, an Officer, was stood in the Green Channel, Terminal Three, watching flight PK787 go through. He was in a good mood, he was having a good run, and the PK787 was one of his favourite flights as he'd had a lot of success from it in the past. He spotted a man who at face value ticked all the boxes. He was travelling alone. He didn't look like he was on business. He didn't look like a returning resident and he seemed a little lost. Added to that, something about him didn't look quite right to Chris.

He didn't fit any of the usual categories of passengers you would expect to see on the PK787.

Chris stopped him. His name was Ahmed. He was, as Chris found out, coming here for the first time and he was visiting relatives. Although strangely enough he didn't have an address. He just said they would be waiting for him outside, but he couldn't say exactly who. He also ticked several other boxes for Chris. It was a brand new passport, this was a good sign. The ticket was cash paid and had cost Mr Ahmed nearly half his annual salary. He was a labourer and labourers do not get paid a lot in Pakistan. He was trying to act relaxed, but he was too relaxed. Chris searched his baggage and realised that the heels on the shoes in his suitcase had all been tampered with. And there were an unusually large number of shoes, all in pairs, but some seemed to be bigger than others. He suspected that they were hollow and had been filled with either cannabis resin, or heroin. He didn't want to delve too deeply because he wanted to run Mr Ahmed and see who he was meeting. He needed to tell someone without alerting Mr Ahmed. He told him stay where he was as he was going to get permission from his Senior Officer to carry out a search of person (SOP). He asked Peter, an Officer we have already met, to keep an eye on him while he spoke to the SO. Chris spoke to the SO and received permission to carry out the SOP. This he did and his suspicions were confirmed when in one of his jacket pockets he found half of a one-hundred Rupee note. He pretended that it was of no interest to him, but he knew the meeter would have the other half, completed the SOP and went back to the bench. Pete knowing just what the score was wandered away and contacted Duggie of the local Investigation Unit and the run was arranged.

Chris had spent a lot of time inspecting the rest of the baggage but avoiding the heels on the shoes. Fortunately for Chris, Ahmed, like a lot of Asian passengers, was carrying all sorts of foodstuffs. So Chris was able to take his time inspecting and testing them. Eventually he got the nod from Pete to say that everyone was in place.

The reader needs to appreciate that back in 1977 HM Customs didn't have too many plain clothes officers, so any uniformed officers who weren't doing anything took off their jacket and tie and put on a civvy jumper or coat to cover up the white shirt and epaulettes.

Chris, Pete, and Brian, another Officer we've met previously, were amongst the followers even though they had all been in and around the Green Channel at the time of the interception and examination. It is amazing how unobservant people can be when they think the pressure is off. There were a dozen officers all watching and waiting all trying to cover his likely avenues of departure. Then he was gone. It was busy in Terminal Three. It always was when a PakAir was around. Most of the people waiting were Pakistanis waiting for relatives. Consequently there were lots of big family groups all waiting to greet friends and relatives. Almost a carnival atmosphere, lots of shouting, cries of delight, people in tears meeting friend or relatives. Not ideal for a run, but off they went. All relatively calm. Ahmed moving about as if he's looking for someone but not really knowing where to go. Then, pandemonium. He had simply disappeared. Chris didn't know what quantity of drugs were in the shoes, in fact he didn't even know what the drugs were. He presumed it was smack. But there were several pairs and they had been put together very professionally so he was guessing there was quite a bit. Too much to lose. Duggie ordered radio silence until he was spotted. There was deafening silence for what seemed like hours, but was probably only a couple of minutes. Then the call they'd all been waiting for. "Target standing by Boots the Chemist".

"Chris proceed to Boots and make a positive ID". This from Duggie.

Another deafening silence then;

"Wrong man, wrong man."

Just when it looked like the whole operation was going sour (tits up is the technical expression) Chris had an enormous bit of luck. Ahmed was spotted coming back into the Terminal from the taxi rank. The officer watching the front of the rank hadn't spotted him, but apparently, they heard this later from the man managing the queue, he had stood in line for about 5 minutes, then he must have realised he was in the wrong place so he picked up his bag and walked off. Chris rushed off to the exit to make another positive ID, and as he was trying to get round a large family group he literally bumped right into him. But again the Gods were on his side. Ahmed was talking to one of the group asking him where to go for the buses, so he didn't recognise him.

The operation was back on track. Although it wouldn't have been a major disaster, it would have been a set-back. These were still relatively early days, and whereas the officers were forever trying to push the boundaries, their Senior Management were not so keen. The loss of Mr Ahmed and his drugs would have given them, the Senior Officers, even more excuse to limit risky operations such as this.

Mr Ahmed was under very close supervision and the officers were emboldened to stay close because of the way he hadn't recognised Chris when he bumped into him. They now followed him to the Bus Station where he boarded a Bus 81B heading for Hounslow West. There were officers on the bus and two cars following the bus. The bus arrived at Hounslow West and Ahmed got off and immediately joined a queue for another bus. The officers didn't know how far to let this go, but Ahmed now seemed to know where he was going so it was decided to let him carry on a bit longer. Anyway all the buses from Hounslow West were local so he wasn't going too far. Sure enough he now jumped on to a 232 bus heading for Southall. That area, with its' large Asian community, was an ideal place for a meet. Nothing could be more natural than two old friends bumping into each other in the street. Ahmed stayed on until the bus reached the Uxbridge Road, a very busy thoroughfare in the middle of Southall. He got off and just ambled up and down for a few minutes. The officers backed off, Ahmed might not be very observant but the person he was meeting might. Also Chris, Pete, and Brian were in very thinly disguised uniform. Chris was Asian so he at least looked like he was in the right place, but Pete and Brian would have stood out like a sore thumb to anyone watching Ahmed. Luckily they didn't have to wait long, it was busy Saturday morning and they were worried he would disappear again amongst the crowds of shoppers. Then all of a sudden, just as they had hoped, a man approached Ahmed and offered his hand. It was just like two old friends meeting up in the street. One did happen to have a suitcase but apart from that, what could be more normal? They started to walk together and the officers gave them time to make sure it wasn't a remarkable coincidence. Just as they moved in the second bloke, who was also Asian, was just in the process of showing Ahmed his half of the one-hundred Rupee note. The timing was perfect. Both men were arrested and returned to Heathrow. When the shoes were taken apart Chris was amazed to find that the heels contained amphetamine. It was the first job of amphetamine that Customs had had up until that date, and it was another indication of how the smugglers were moving on. It was also a very strange importation, because at this time amphetamine was produced in this country and we were a major exporter, illegal exporter that is, to Europe and the USA.

Ahmed's lack of awareness might seem strange. But it was not unique. The adrenalin is pumping, he's not the fizziest drink in the fridge, he's not the type of professional courier we will meet in later years, and he's in a strange country. Add to that the Officer has seen his half hundred rupee note, which might give him away, but he's shown no interest. On one occasion an Officer called Len followed a suspect around Terminal 4, for 45 minutes. He actually bumped into him on three occasions. However when he was finally arrested the man not only wasn't aware he'd been followed, he refused to believe it. Even when Len was able to refer to his notebook and give every detail of where he'd been within the Terminal, he still didn't believe it. He was so wrapped up in what he was doing he was completely oblivious to the fact that he was being followed by Len who was in full uniform except for a casual jacket.

**

Stranger than Fiction

Some drug detections and the circumstances around the detection beggar belief. Sometimes there is no good explanation for what happens, but sometimes something that appears inexplicable is explained when the whole truth is established. On the face of it they are stranger than fiction.

**

It was a Thursday and Drew was stood watching the passengers from Mombasa filter into the Reclaim Hall. The bags were beginning to appear on the baggage belt. Drew was having a mediocre sort of day. That's the sort of chap he was. Not too many highs and not too many lows. He just jogged along and got on with the job. Little did he know he was just about to set in motion one of the most bizarre sets of events ever to come to the attention of HM Customs at Heathrow.

Drew wasn't actually that interested in the Kenya Airways flight. It was a sort of medium risk flight which sometimes produced and sometimes it didn't. The team were waiting for the Kingston and he'd been sent ahead to let the rest of the team know when it started to come into the Hall. However while he was stood there waiting he did notice two bright pink hard sided Samsonite suitcases going round and round on the reclaim belt. Nothing suspicious in that, just a bit unusual. Back in the day suitcases carrying drugs tended to be very nondescript and boring, just like the vast majority of suitcases. If there were several similar suitcases on a flight it gave the miscreant a chance to claim that he had picked up the wrong suitcase. These two Samsonites certainly weren't boring.

Drew was watching, well sort of watching, but not very interested in, the passengers congregate around the belt. In fact he was really just pointed in the general direction of the Reclaim Belt. Obviously this was way back in history as the bags had actually arrived before the passengers. He then noticed a little chap walking down the stairs from Immigration. This man just didn't look right. He didn't look like any of the groups of people you would normally expect to see on a Mombasa. Passenger groups tend to wear their own types of uniforms. Holiday makers tend to look the same, business men the same, etc. On the Mombasa flights there were five distinct groups. There were holiday makers, ex pats (that is UK residents who had immigrated to Kenya in the recent past), business men, people who had lived there for generations, and lastly Civil Servants. They all had their own type of uniform, but the man Drew was looking at didn't fit into any of these groups. In fact he looked more like Del Boy, straight out of Only Fools and Horses. If he'd been arriving on a Brussels or Paris then Drew wouldn't have looked at him twice

Drew watched Del Boy approach the belt and pick up the two bright pink Samsonite suitcases. He then proceeded to push his trolley into the Green Channel where he was intercepted by Drew.

Drew went through the normal questioning and he soon established that Del Boy lived in the UK, he was from Harold Hill in Essex, he was an OAP, and he had no good reason for travel. Although he did say it was for a holiday, but he was obviously not a holiday maker, he couldn't even remember the name of his hotel. He had the infamous cash paid ticket, and later it transpired that he had a CRO. That is, he had been in prison four or five times for housebreaking and burglary.

When the two suitcases were opened they were found to be full of compressed herbal cannabis. Absolutely full, no clothes, an empty pillowcase on the top of each one, but otherwise nothing else at all. Using Customs vernacular, a "bagful". In fact two bagsful.

Del Boy was of course amazed.

"Ow did that get there?" He wanted to know.

"Where have all me clothes gone?" He also wanted to know.

"Actually," said Drew, "I'm the one who asks the questions."

Despite making no admissions and maintaining his amazement, Del Boy was eventually charged. He couldn't explain how the cannabis got there, where his clothes were, who might have put it there etc. He had been on holiday he claimed. He didn't look like he had. There was nothing on his person or in his hand baggage to suggest he had. He couldn't remember the name of the hotel. Amazingly he couldn't remember where he'd bought his magnificent suitcases. He was taken before Uxbridge Magistrates, and granted bail. Nothing too unusual so far. Two bagsful, unusual for there to be two, but not that unusual. The pink suitcases were a bit bizarre but hardly worthy of being classed as stranger than fiction! But what followed definitely was.

Same scenario a fortnight later. This time there's a whole team stood at the front of the Green. They're watching the Kingston passengers filter down from the Immigration Lounge, and standing round Belt 6,which is directly adjacent to the mouth of the Green in Terminal Three, waiting for their bags which are probably being given a good looking at out the back by the Tarmac teams and the dogs.

The Mombasa was already in the Hall and the bags were beginning to bump along Belt 8, about 40 yards down the Hall. Suddenly one of the team, a bit more eagle eyed than the rest, or maybe he wasn't concentrating on the Kingston, spotted a bright pink hard sided suitcase. He nudged the Officer next to him and nodded towards Belt 8. Then, as the two of them were watching it another one appeared. Now this was too much of a coincidence, so the two of them peeled off and took up a position to watch the Mombasa passengers.

Sure enough five minutes later a Del Boy lookalike came trotting down the stairs. He picked up the two suitcases and headed for the Green. The two Officers intercepted him and the same story unravelled. Lived in the UK, Romford, had been away on holiday, he was an OAP, he had a cash paid ticket and he had a CRO. He also was amazed when the suitcases were opened and were found to contain nothing but compressed herbal cannabis. He wanted to know who had put all that "herbie" stuff in his suitcases. He's obviously spoken to his mate as he could give the name of the hotel he had supposedly stayed at. This of course rebounded on him as were able to prove he hadn't stayed there. He was eventually charged, taken to Uxbridge and granted bail. So that was the end of that.

Oh no it wasn't. A fortnight later, same day, a Thursday, same Kenya Airways flight from Mombasa. Same two bright pink hard sided suitcases. Same Del Boy lookalike. Exactly the same set of circumstances. This was getting silly. Surely whoever was behind this was getting the message.

Not at all, nobody was getting the message. Another two weeks later the same thing. In fact every two weeks for three months a Del Boy lookalike from the Harold Hill area of Essex was apprehended bringing in two pink suitcases full of compressed herbal cannabis.

But why? All the men were getting bail, so presumably they were getting back home and relaying what had occurred to the men behind it all. Eventually one of the old lags did talk, and a young man about 35 years of age was brought in for questioning. He admitted to being involved with the last importation but denied knowledge of the previous attempts. Despite his denials he did at one point ask the interviewing Officer.

"Ow come you kept 'nickin' ma boys?"

"It was like shooting fish in a barrel", came the prompt reply. "But what do you mean all your boys. What other boys. I thought you didn't know anything about previous attempts?"

The puzzle was never solved. Why were the men behind it all prepared to let a sacrificial lamb go down once a fortnight for three months? Was it a diversion? Unlikely. The old lags wouldn't have been happy about going back inside just to let someone else get through. But also how could they be sure that we would pick up the first consignment, and why use two suitcases. If it was a diversion one bag would have been enough to grab the officers' attention. Also why a bagful. A small package in a pink suitcase would have been enough. Most likely the old lags were prepared to take a chance, possibly they all had some money invested. If they managed to get one shipment through then everything would be covered. Why didn't they change the colour of the suitcases? Well the providers didn't give a damn if they kept getting caught. The old boys wouldn't have had a chance to move the drugs to different baggage as the cases wouldn't have been delivered until shortly before they were on their way to the airport on their way home. But also of course, more importantly, as they were old lags they weren't bothered if they ended up doing time. At their age they would almost certainly end up in an Open Prison somewhere in Essex, near enough for friends and relatives to visit. They'd probably have weekends off, only going back if they felt like it, days out, Sky TV in their cells. To men who'd done the amount of time that these chaps had it wasn't really a deterrent. The thirty five year old, who continually referred to "his boys", who were all old enough to be his grandfather, ended up in the Scrubs. And miraculously, after his arrest the shipments ceased. Or maybe, and this is a scary thought. They just changed the colour of the suitcases.

**

The pink suitcases were bizarre but it wasn't unusual for drug smugglers to use a series of identical suitcases or in this case trunks.

It was very early and Mike was stood in the Green Channel, Terminal Three, chatting to Chris who we've seen before, and a Dave who we haven't. They were on the seven AM to three PM watch and they were just getting into their stride for the day. As usual in Terminal Three first thing in the morning it was very very busy. All the Far East flights were around and some from West Africa. The Ghana Airways flight from Accra was down and they were all just standing there chatting and watching. It was a high risk flight but the mood was very relaxed. They'd been having a good run and there was no pressure. As they stood there watching a

Ghanaian man pushed his trolley past them. On the trolley was a great big black metal trunk decorated with brightly coloured half-moons on the side. The trunk took up the whole of the trolley and was probably about four feet long and two feet wide. Chris half-jokingly said to Dave.

"There's a nice job going by."

He didn't make any move to stop the man so Dave had to race down the Green Channel after him. Now this was no mean feat as Dave could never be described as willowy and he wasn't prone to sudden bursts of energy. But on this occasion he moved with remarkable speed for such a large chap. Dave went through the normal questions, he was getting a good feel about this as the man was being very evasive about his length of stay, where he was going to stay, why he was here, and who he was meeting. Dave asked him directly when he was returning to Ghana. The man just shrugged. Dave wondered if he should involve HM Immigration. Judging by the size of the trunk he was going to be here for some time. Maybe he was thinking of making it a permanent move. In fact Dave gained the impression that he wasn't exactly being evasive he just didn't know the answers to any of these questions. He was acting very strangely. It was almost as if every now and then he had to remind himself to act calmly.

Eventually Dave decided to open the trunk. When he did he found the usual hotchpotch of clothing and personal belongings. Lots of foul smelling foodstuff. Then two thirds of the way down the trunk he came across the biggest double bottom to a piece of baggage he had ever seen. In fact it was probably the biggest double bottom that any officer had ever seen. It was about a foot deep. Not very subtle. It was just a sheet of metal being kept down by the weight of the food. When the sheet of metal was removed lo and behold it was full of herbal cannabis.

Now up to this point it was a very straight forward job which was just how the not very willowy Dave liked it. But it soon became very complicated. Dave was joined by Mike and Chris and another Dave, who we will call little Dave, otherwise it might get very confusing. There were a lot of

Daves around back then. Little Dave looked at the trunk and thought he had seen something similar sitting by one of the reclaim belts. He nipped back to the Reclaim Hall, but the trunk wasn't there. So he popped along to British Airways Lost and Found area where unclaimed baggage was kept for three days before being taken to their main warehouse. Sure enough there was an identical black metal trunk decorated with little brightly coloured half-moons. On investigation this trunk was also found to have a very crude false bottom containing cannabis. Now normally with mishandled baggage, as the airlines liked to call baggage that they had managed to lose for some unsuspecting passenger, that was the end of the trail. If there was C1422, that is a written declaration, then normally, for obvious reasons, it showed a false address. However on this occasion, miraculously, there was an address, just down the road in Hounslow, and it eventually turned out to be genuine.

Little Dave was now quite agitated, of course at this stage they hadn't apprehended the second punter, but he had a trunk with approximately 10 kilos of cannabis. Although not given to great displays of emotion he was obviously very pleased with himself. However this slightly complicated job was about to get more complicated. While little Dave and Chris were trying to decide the best way to follow this up, one of the BA Lost and Found staff remembered a passenger who had come to their desk looking for a trunk with half-moons on the side. They had eventually traced the trunk to the Freight Sheds on the North side of the airport and had sent him on his way to go and find it. So now Chris decided that these complications were a bit too much for them to handle. Going and picking up a punter from an address in Hounslow and linking him to a trunk covered in half-moons was one thing. But tracing a trunk in the Freight sheds and following that up was an entirely different kettle of fish. So the Investigation Unit were invited to become involved. This they did with alacrity. Although it was only cannabis they were having a bit of a slow time and this obviously had potential. It would also get them out of the office. They could go spinning drums as they called it. Translated to you and I, that means searching houses. They loved spinning drums. They would spin them until they were quite dizzy.

The Unit eventually traced the trunk that had gone to the Freight sheds. And again amazingly they had another real address, also in Hounslow. They then proceeded to both houses and rounded up the punters numbered two and three. Number one being the one in the Green Channel. They found the trunk belonging to number three, but minus the cannabis. So they brought the whole lot back to Terminal Three and handed them over to the Officers." Not so willowy" Dave's uncomplicated job was now a three hander and it hadn't stopped growing.

The three clients are now safely ensconced in three interview rooms and the three interviews are being carried out by "not so willowy" Dave, little Dave, and Chris. There's lots of toing and froing going on between the rooms because the Officers want to tie all three of them to all three importations. There's about 15 kilos in each trunk and the officers want to charge all three of them with the attempted fraudulent evasion of 45 kilos not 15 kilos each. They are trying to do this even though 15 kilos are missing. If they can get admissions then they can be included even though they aren't actually there. Or maybe they might even get the address where they are. But this is unlikely. As client number three is having the two names of clients one and two put to him, he gets himself in a muddle. Either that or he doesn't know them very well, and he refers to client number two by a completely different name. The Officers now realise that there is a fourth metal trunk with brightly coloured half-moons lurking around somewhere. But where is it? It's not on today's Accra flight, the one from yesterday has been found in the Lost and Found. The one from the day before yesterday has been located after it went to the Freight Village. So was there one from the day before that? Or is there one coming tomorrow? The riddle was never solved. It was probably due the following day. But aborted when the news filtered back to Ghana that the previous runs had failed. The three Officers did an amazing job in getting all three tied in together. All three were charged with the 45 kilos and as a consequence received far lengthier sentences from the Judge at Isleworth than they would have if they'd been charged separately.

**

An Officer, we'll call him Ollie, previously seen rugby tackling Leroy Winston Montereaux, was in the Green Channel, Terminal Three, and he was having a bad day. He wasn't feeling too good from the night before and his Senior Officer was giving him grief. He had been at a do the night before at London Scottish Rugby Club, full of Posh Jocks as Ollie described them. Ollie, he of the outrageously predictable "dummy" was particularly elated about the whole affair, as he had got to meet Frans ten Bos a legend of Scottish rugby. So he was keeping his head down stopping the odd passenger but not really wanting to find anything. This was unusual because Ollie was a good Officer with a good record of finding drugs.

Reg, who wasn't on his Team, was in the Green Channel with him, and was keeping half an eye on him as he obviously wasn't in good shape. Reg had known Ollie since before they both came to Heathrow. They had worked together at LOMO, opening parcels. Finding cannabis inside cakes and small bits of coke in toothpaste tubes, things like that. So they knew one another quite well. In fact on one occasion they had between them, broken up a fight on the platform at West Ham Tube Station. They still laughed about one of the lads involved who wanted to keep fighting because as he said, he liked getting hurt. No accounting for what turns certain people on. Anyway back to the story. Reg was actually worried that Ollie might emulate an Officer who years ago, so the story went, had actually fallen asleep in a passengers' case whilst examining it. Apparently the lid was up so the passenger hadn't realised for a while that the Officer was asleep. It was only when he started snoring that he looked over the lid and found an unconscious officer having a little siesta in amongst his dirty underwear. So Reg is paying more attention watching Ollie than he is looking at the passengers.

At this point the South African airways flight is coming through. Not a high risk flight at the time. A bit of cannabis, not a lot, just small amounts. Ollie's not really interested in the South African so he's not actually stopping anyone. Then as he's stood there an IC1 man of about forty years of age comes up to him. He's pushing a trolley with two hard sided suitcases on it. He's smart, looks like a business man, and he thrusts his

Passport at Ollie and tells him he's South African. Now Ollie doesn't really care where he's from. He could be from outer space for all he cares. But he takes the Passport and pretends to be interested. It'll keep his SO off of his back for a few minutes.

Ollie goes through the usual questions. The man's name was Botha, it rang a bell with Ollie because a certain Mr Naas Botha was the South African fly half at the time. Not related as it turned out. He lived in Pretoria and he was coming here for five days for a business meeting. Ollie is now off of autopilot. And this is where he shows his true worth. Bad as he's feeling he can't help wondering why would he need two large suitcases if he's only here for 5 days?

"Where are you going after you leave this country?"

"Back to South Africa."

So no need for lots of clothing.

"What sort of business are you in?"

"Mining, coal mining."

So he's not going to have a suitcase full of samples.

"Are you carrying any merchandise with you, or anything to do with your business trip?"

"No just a few papers."

Ollie now notices that Mr Botha is getting very red and has started to sweat.

He is very calm which would normally be seen as a sign that maybe he's up to something. Most people when they're stopped aren't calm. They don't know how to act to convince the Officer that they're innocent of any wrong doing. So nine times out of ten innocent people act very nervous and uncomfortable. But as has been said previously people who are up to something overdo the calmness in their efforts to appear unconcerned and relaxed. But this isn't a normal situation because Ollie didn't actually stop Mr Botha. Mr Botha offered himself up as a sacrificial lamb. So although he's very calm he's getting redder and redder. Ollie now notices that his passenger is wearing a raincoat and it's fully done up.

"Do you want to take your coat off?" Asks Ollie.

"No, I'm fine."

He doesn't look fine. By now even Reg has noticed how red he is. Again this is where Oliie shows what a good Officer he is. He's still feeling terrible but he now thinks he's on to something. He gets Mr Botha to sit on the bench because he's now as red as the proverbial beetroot and he's sweating profusely. But he still won't take off his raincoat. He asks Reg to give him a hand. The suitcases are locked and Mr Botha can't remember what he's done with the keys. "Amazingly" Reg has a Samsonite key on his key ring. It's the most common of the Samsonite locks and after a bit of manipulation it's open.

The two Officers are now so worried about Mr Botha that Reg goes off to get a glass of water. When he comes back into the Green Channel, the first thing he notices is that Ollie seems to have taken a leaf out of story of Lazarus. He has risen from the dead. No sign of his hangover now. He is just standing there looking at Reg with a great big grin, but a slightly confused look on his face.

Reg gives the glass to Mr Botha who has actually assumed a slightly less red colour. He turns to Ollie who just points to the suitcase. The suitcase is now empty, and Reg can see the biggest false bottom to a suitcase that he's ever seen. But it's empty. There are no drugs. The second case is opened and it's the same story. A massive concealment but with no drugs. The two Officers are now looking very closely at Mr Botha, and you don't have to be a rocket scientist to guess what they're thinking. Ollies' SO who has been hovering around all morning is now absent. Now they need him to get permission for a Search of Person he's nowhere to be seen. Typical, SO's are like buses and policemen, but in reverse. There's normally two or three getting in the way when you don't need them, then as soon as you do need one you can't find one for love or money. But eventually they find him and he gives permission for a strip search. They escort Mr Botha into the search room. He's not saying a word. His rights are explained and a note is opened in the SOP Register. He takes off his raincoat and gives it to Ollie. He nearly drops it. It is so heavy. There are two large packages in two deep inside pockets. Mr Botha is still saying nothing. The Officers now look at Mr Botha, and Mr Botha is, putting it mildly, looking a little bit lumpy. His suit jacket is removed and strapped round his middle and under his arms are another three packages. When his trousers are removed there's another package stuffed into his underpants. They open one of the packages, and it contains compressed herbal cannabis. The smell gives it away and the Field Test confirms it. When it's all weighed it weighs just under twelve kilos. It's amazing he could walk. No wonder he was so red and was sweating. The two Officers are shaking their heads in disbelief. This is going to be one hell of a story when they finally get to the bottom of it.

Mr Botha is arrested and escorted to an Interview Room and, under Caution and on tape, the story unfolds. Mr Botha is not a dealer. But he has friend who lives over here in the UK and who uses pot on a regular basis. Every time he goes home to South Africa he picks up a few kilos because it's better quality and cheaper than what he's buying in Maida Vale. He and Mr Botha have actually travelled together on one occasion while his friend was carrying, and this has proved how easy it is. So Mr Botha is persuaded by his friend to bring over twelve kilos. Six for his friend and six that his friend can sell to his friends at quite a profit. His friend gives him two suitcases, suitably adapted, that he will keep and use on his next trip to London. He packs six kilos in each suitcase. All of this does suggest the friend was a lot more involved than he was letting on. People importing primarily for personal use don't normally go in for double bottomed suitcases. The trouble is that Mr Botha really hasn't got the nerve for this sort of thing. He checks in at Johannesburg and is worried that the check in girl seems more diligent than normal. He doesn't remember being asked some of the questions on previous trips. All the time he's in the airport he feels like he's being watched. He keeps asking Ollie and Reg:-

"I was being watched wasn't I?"

"You were onto me even then weren't you?"

This man has obviously read too many James Bond thrillers.

Even on the flight he feels like the stewards are watching him. When they land he's held up in Immigration. He isn't, just the normal queues, but he thinks he is. There's no problem with his Passport. He still feels he's being watched. His paranoia is now so bad that he knows he's been rumbled. But of course he hasn't. His suitcases arrive and he can see that they have been tampered with. They haven't, but he's sure they have. He now just doesn't know what to do. If they, that is Customs, know there's drugs in the suitcase, then if he goes through the Green they will see the suitcases and stop him and the game will be up. So he decides to go to the toilets, remove the drugs and hide them on his person. Then dump the suitcase and just walk through. He thinks if he dumps the suitcases with the drugs in they will be traced to him and he will be caught. He goes to one of the airline desks without his bags and asks to borrow some tape because his case is damaged. They just give it to him. Considering the state he's in this is remarkably brave of him. He goes to the toilet and gets in a cubicle with the suitcases. It must have been one hell of a squeeze. He removes the drugs, hides them about his person, and is going to leave the suitcases in the toilet but he can't. He tries to leave the cubicle without them but he's been so long in the cubicle there is now a massive queue, as there's only two cubicles. So he wheels the suitcases out into the Reclaim Hall. He just can't find anywhere to leave them. He walks into the mouth of the Green

Channel then he turns round and goes back into the Reclaim Hall. Then he summons all his courage and walks back into the Green Channel. And then in his words:-

"You (Ollie) were looking straight at me. I knew you knew. I knew you were waiting for me to try and get through. I could tell by the look on your face. So I decided to come clean."

"So why didn't you tell me straight away?"

"Well when you spoke you seemed so sort of distant, kind of faraway. I was beginning to think that maybe you didn't know, maybe you weren't well, and I might get away with it."

Little did he know that Ollie looking "distant" was something to do with the time he'd spent with the London Scottish the night before. And had he just kept walking he probably would have walked straight through.

Sadly for him, a man of previous good character, with no reason to get involved in drugs, ended up before Reading Crown Court, and doing time at Her Majesty's Pleasure. Doubly sadly nothing could be pinned on the "friend", and he escaped scot-free.

**

Saleem Qadir Qazi thought he had covered every angle and had come up with a way of smuggling drugs that would leave him in the clear even if the drugs were found.

Flight PK785 from Islamabad was in the Reclaim Hall and the Green Channel in Terminal Three was full of Officers. There were two teams from Terminal Three, there was an Enforcement Team, there were Investigating Officers hovering around. They wouldn't actually stop passengers but they would follow up any potential runs, they weren't in uniform, and they were trained in covert watching and following techniques. The Tarmac boys were out the back and there were two drug dogs running around over the suitcases before they reached the belt. This was a high risk flight and just recently it had been very productive for heroin. The Duty Senior Officer, Dennis, was everywhere, making sure that everyone was firing on all cylinders. He really didn't need to bother, everyone was on their toes. The Pakair was one of those flights where the Officers knew there was always going to be something on it. There was just the small matter of picking the right passenger and then the problem of finding it. This could be tricky as normally there were masses of bags. But at least they knew there was a good chance that there would be something somewhere.

Mo, a North Londoner who was on Denis's team was having a good run. He wasn't seen as one of the "Seizure Kings", but he was a good steady Officer who always hit his targets. The sort of Officer you could rely on, the sort you would describe as the backbone of the Department.

The passengers were now coming through. As ever with the Pakair there were lots of large family groups, these were always difficult for Officers because there was so little to go on. They were normally British Pakistanis who lived in the UK and had been back to Pakistan for a holiday, a family wedding, or maybe a funeral. This meant they had a real reason for travel so 99% of what they would be telling the Officer would be the truth. This made it difficult for the Officer to decide if it was worth going through a whole load of baggage for nothing. It was getting very busy. There wasn't the normal charge of people pushing their trolleys because the Tarmac boys and the dogs were doing a thorough job out the back. There had already been one dog indication and the Enforcement Team and two of the Investigators were dealing with that. It was getting busy and yet again the air conditioning was malfunctioning so it was getting hot.

Mo had stopped one couple, but he let them proceed without searching their luggage. He then spotted Saleem Qazi. He was pushing his trolley with a large black suitcase and a cardboard box on it. He wasn't hanging around, he was moving very quickly down the Channel. Straightaway Mo thought he ticked a lot of the boxes. He was on his own, he looked like he lived in this country, and he fitted the profile of a recent run of heroin smugglers from the sub-Continent. Men, aged between forty and sixty, obviously living here from their dress, travelling alone, smuggling between half a kilo and whole kilo of very pure heroin. They all lived in the Southall, Heston, Hayes, Hounslow area close to Heathrow. Somebody had set up a nice little cottage industry. Not too big, just keeping below the radar. Qazi was moving so fast Mo had to actually chase after him. He caught up with him about three quarters of the way down the Channel and guided him to the bench. Qazi was calm! Was he too calm, Mo asked himself? He spoke reasonable English although he definitely wasn't fluent. Mo established that he lived here, in Colham Green right next door to Hayes. He had been back to Pakistan to see his family. He mentioned a little village that Mo had never heard of. Somewhere up in the mountains near to Peshawar. Mo looked at his Passport which was old and showed two or three trips back home. His ticket was cash paid but they often were in these circumstances. Very often families scraped their money together and bought their tickets from Bucket shops in the Uxbridge Road. Qazi agreed it was his suitcase which he had packed himself, the box contained mangos. This was a bit odd because back then mangos were more associated with India rather than Pakistan. However Qazi said he had bought them in a market in Islamabad just before his departure, and Mo was quite happy they didn't have anything in them.

Mo looked up. He said later that if he'd seen a better bet he might well have let Qazi proceed. There wasn't anyone better, and Dennis the SO, was hovering around so he decided to carry on. Mo had a quick look at the Baggage Tag and checked the number against the counterfoil on the ticket. They were the same. Qazi put the suitcase on the bench and opened it.

This was when things went a bit strange. Mo found himself looking at a suitcase full of women's clothing. He looked at Qazi who was looking at the clothing with a dazed expression on his face.

"Are these your clothes"? Asked a very confused Mo.

Qazi shrugged.

"No don't just shrug, are these your clothes or are you carrying them for someone else?"

Qazi it appeared could no longer speak any English. Mo had already established that he was travelling alone.

Qazi shrugged again.

"Have you been asked to bring these clothes over for someone?"

"No understand", said Qazi.

This, as it transpired was true. Qazi was reeling with the shock of seeing what he thought was his suitcase full of these female clothes. He really didn't understand.

Mo's first thought was that maybe he was dealing with a cross dresser. And he didn't mean an irate piece of bedroom furniture. He hadn't met a cross dresser from Pakistan before and he wasn't too sure how it would fit with the Muslim faith, but it did appear to be a distinct possibility. Since coming to Heathrow and looking in peoples suitcases, and having previously worked on ships, he had come to realise just how many people got up to strange practices in the privacy of their own homes. So he decided to have a look in the toilette bag which was near the top of the suitcase. It was a pretty bag with little pink flowers, very feminine. Mo had worked it out that even if Qazi was a cross dresser he would need shaving gear. He looked into the bag. There were all the usual pots and tubes that you would expect in a ladies toilette bag. But no razor, no shaving brush, no shaving cream. Mo had emptied a few of the pots of cream out of the bag and noticed that the nearly empty bag was unusually heavy. He emptied the rest out and it was still heavy. It was too heavy. As he held it he noticed that the bottom of it was quite thick and stiff. He teased the lining away with his lock-knife. Underneath he could just see the brown tape much beloved by drug smugglers. He didn't disturb it, not wanting to ruin any finger print evidence, but he knew it was drugs, almost certainly heroin. This type of concealment meant he had to look in every conceivable hiding place in the suitcase, and on Qazis person. He wasn't disappointed. In a small blue powder bowl he found more twists covered with brown tape, and in two Elvive shampoo bottles he found ten more twists of heroin. Later it would be established that there was a total of nine-hundred grams of heroin at 75% purity. Not an earth shattering amount, but a nice little earner if done regularly enough. It all fitted perfectly with the recent trend.

At this point Mo asked Mike (the Alfred E Newman lookalike who we last saw dealing with the Jamaican lady with the happy pussy) to accompany him into the box with Qazi. Mo should have known better, but to be fair nobody could have anticipated the conversation that ensued.

Mo had written up his official Notebook with the events up to this point. He then had to read what he had written to Qazi to get him to agree or disagree his account. This also gave the jockey a chance to know the details of what was going on. A decent jockey was worth their weight in gold. The Case Officer would often get so personally involved that they couldn't see the wood for the trees. Whereas the jockey could sit back with much more of an overview and see the flaws in the suspects' replies. But of course to do this he had to know what had been said and done in the Green.

So Mo started in the normal way.

"At approximately so and so time on such and such date I stopped the person I now know to be Mr Saleem Qadir Qazi, in the Green Channel, Terminal Three."

At which point Qazi said, "no". Just like that, nothing else simply, "no".

"What do you mean, no?" Asked Mo.

Mo looked at the passport. He hadn't been mistaken. The name was Saleem Qazi, and the picture was definitely of the man standing in front of him.

"Are you saying that this is not your passport?" Asked Mo.

"This is my passport, yes it is my passport."

"I am not a Qazi I am a Qazee", said Qazi pronouncing it Carzee.

There was a silence, Mo looked at Mike who was suddenly all ears, and not just physically all ears, he was really listening. Qazi was pronouncing his surname the way we pronounce the word khazi as slang for a toilet. If that wasn't bad enough Qazi insisted on repeating this statement several times. "I am a Carzee" he kept saying. Mo had to get this straight as he wouldn't want to be seen to be mocking Qazi during the interview.

"So your name is pronounced Carzee?" He said.

"Yes", said Qazi, "I am a Carzee".

He, Qazi, then repeated this four or five times.

"I am a Carzee", he kept saying.

Not Mr Carzee, not Saleem Carzee, no he was A Carzee. There was no doubt about it, he was insisting that he was a toilet.

Mo found out later that around Peshwar there were different tribes or clans who pronounced their names differently and Qazi wanted to make quite sure that there was no mistake about who he belonged to. It turned out that the Carzees thought they were a cut above Qazis which is why he was so insistent. Mo was trying not look at Mike as he knew exactly what would be going through his mind. After the fourth or fifth repetition Mike could restrain himself no longer. He looked Qazi straight in the eye and said in a deadly serious voice.

"Well Mo I think it's fair to say that normally in this country the crap is in the khazi, but on this occasion it looks like the khazi is in the crap." This was all on the tape so needless to say the Defence made an absolute meal out of this when Mike was in the Witness Box at Isleworth Crown Court.

Mo was struggling. Every time he questioned Qazi about the contents of the case he said he didn't understand. It obviously wasn't his suitcase, but had he been given a suitcase without knowing what it contained, and just told to deliver it. Very unlikely. If it was someone else's and he had picked it up by mistake why didn't he just say so? Mike had been back to the belt in case it was a switch bag routine, but there were no similar bags around. A couple of the others on the team had been out to the Concourse but there was nobody carrying a similar case out there. Or so they thought. It was very busy and it was full of large groups of Pakistani families meeting relatives. The airline passenger list was checked, and to all intents and purposes it looked like Qazi was travelling alone.

Mo could see a good Defence Brief getting a not guilty on this one, and he was convinced Qazi was complicit in the smuggling attempt. His English was getting worse and worse, and there were more and more "no understands", and more and more, "no replies".

At this point Mike, who was as sharp as he was funny, was re-examining all the bits of paperwork. Then he noticed a discrepancy between the Baggage Tag and the counterfoil attached to the ticket. One was PK 88898899 and one was PK 88898989. This didn't help, it appeared to prove Qazis' innocence. So why wasn't he jumping up and down claiming it wasn't his bag. It didn't make sense.

The passenger list was checked again and the bag was shown to be the property of a young lady with a different family name. Obviously not related. The Concourse outside was searched again, but without result. She wasn't upstairs at Immigration so she presumably had been landed. A quick check with the airline. No she hadn't reported a missing bag. So where was she, why hadn't she reported it when her bag wasn't on the Reclaim belt, and where was Qazis' bag?

Even when Mo went back over the Green Channel questions.

"Do you agree that in the Green Channel you told me this was your bag?"

A nod.

"And do you agree you told me you had packed it yourself?"

No reply.

"If this is the suitcase you checked in can you tell me why the Tag and the Counterfoil are different?"

No reply.

"Can I assume that when you told me it was your suitcase you were mistaken, or were you lying?"

"No understand."

Mo was beginning to think that not only would he be found not guilty, he was beginning to think that there was a good chance he wouldn't even be charged.

Then just when all seemed lost. An amazing stupendous stroke of luck. It was already a strange situation, but it now became stranger than fiction. During a break in questioning Mike left the room to organise some teas. He grabbed Rich, a particularly idle AO who was sitting around doing nothing and sent him up to the canteen to get four teas (the Solicitor had now arrived) and some biscuits. The AO took his time, it was a chance to get out of the office. So rather than go straight upstairs to the canteen, he wandered around and went through to the Departures Lounge, he wanted to see a mate of his who was working on the VAT Refund desk. As he walked in the direction of Departures he passed the Meeting Point. As the name suggests this is a designated area for people to meet. He looked over and he couldn't help but notice an absolutely stunning young Pakistani girl. She was dressed in traditional dress and she looked about eighteen. Even though Rich didn't normally go for women if they weren't westernised, he thought she was gorgeous, and he couldn't help loitering to get a proper look at her. She was just sat there quite calm without a care in the world. Rich went through saw his mate, then he went for the teas. Eventually he returned to the Interview Room. Mike asked him if he'd had to go to Assam for the tea. He had been a long time but Mike's sarcasm was lost on him as he didn't have a clue where Assam was and didn't know that they grew tea there. To try and change the subject as he could tell Mo in particular was not very happy with him, he remarked that he had just seen an identical suitcase to the one in corner. The gorgeous young girl had a similar suitcase and although he definitely hadn't been looking at her suitcase it must have registered somewhere in the recesses of his idle mind.

To say it had the desired effect is certainly an understatement of great magnitude. They certainly weren't worried about his tardiness now.

"What do you mean identical suitcase, where, when, who, how?"

Rich spluttered out the details. He didn't know what had been going on so he didn't realise the gold dust that he had just sprinkled around. The look on Qazis' face was a picture. The only people who didn't have a clue what was going on were Rich and the Solicitor. For Qazi it was the beginning of the end.

The young lady was retrieved from the Meeting Point. Her brand new Passport showed that she was not called Qazi. She had no tag on her ticket so presumably Qazi had removed it to confuse things further. When opened it was full of men's clothes. The case was searched but no more heroin was found. She genuinely spoke no English so an interpreter was brought in. Eventually the story came out. Qazi had been to Pakistan and married the young lady using the name Qureshi. She was being used as an unknowing mule. Qazi planted the drugs in her suitcase and arranged with her to come through separately. It never came out just what he'd told her to explain this. The plan was that he would go through first. If he was stopped he had nothing and he was returning from a trip to Pakistan to see his family in a small village near Peshawar. He would be allowed through and he would wait outside for her, presumably at the Meeting Point. She would come through later. If she was stopped, he would wait around for a bit then leave her to it. They had checked in slightly apart so the tag numbers weren't consecutive, and they were using different family names. For him it was foolproof. Except it wasn't, and although the tag numbers weren't consecutive they were very similar. They were about ten numbers long, nearly all eights and nines, one ended eight nine and one ended nine eight, so it was easy to mistake one for another. Especially with adrenalin pumping through his veins. And that is exactly what he'd done and so had Mo when he compared them in the Green. Presumably Qazi had either destroyed or sent home the passport with his other name on it.

Hence Qazis' amazement when Mo opened the suitcase and revealed his wife's clothing. He genuinely was confused. But he couldn't say it wasn't his suitcase. If he had he would have been taken back to the Reclaim Belt to find his. The real owner of the dirty suitcase would have been found and the story would have come out. He had to play for time and hope that his wife would not be found. And but for an idle Assistant Officer with an over-active libido he would have got away with it. Perhaps he should have picked a less attractive girl to marry.

Eventually both were charged with Attempted Fraudulent Evasion of the Prohibition. However although Qazi now claimed no knowledge of the contents of his wife's suitcase, the jury found him guilty and her not guilty. So there is justice in this world. She obviously was the innocent party and really didn't have a clue what was going on.

As the saying goes: you couldn't make it up, and in instances like this you don't have to.

**

Officers in Court

Going to Court could be the most traumatic experience for officers. Invariably the Defending Counsel would try to cast doubt upon the honesty or the inefficiency of the officers involved. Very often it was their only defence. In the late seventies Bill, a Senior Officer based in Terminal Three, would make himself available to Officers who were due to make their first appearance in Court and later there would be very realistic training that would put officers through the experience before they ever set foot in a Witness Box. Some officers found this training more harrowing than the real thing as they were being judged by their peers. When you eventually went to Court there were several cardinal rules:

Call the Judge 'Your Honour'.

Always address the jury.

If you made a mistake, admit it.

Never give opinions unless directed to by the Judge. You always did what the Judge said.

If there is a discrepancy between your notebook and Witness Statement, the notebook, which would have been written at the time, is correct. Unless of course there are three other notebooks also all made up at the time which say you are wrong.

Never say it was because of information received. If asked just look at the Prosecuting Counsel he should object to the judge. In most cases the judge will uphold the objection. If the judge overrules the objection Customs will withdraw the case. They never want the opposition to know that it was the result of information as this can open a whole bag of worms. So they refuse to answer. If they only refused when the answer was yes then it would be obvious to all, and the same can of worms would be opened.

Never claim to be an expert. If you do, the defence will pull you apart. "I am not an expert but I do have some knowledge on the subject", was the stock answer.

Look professional sound professional.

Don't fence with the Defence.

Don't show exasperation. (Very difficult at times).

Don't smile, unless it's the Judge who makes the joke.

It was a veritable minefield and Officers showed their true mettle when in court.

**

When the Defence felt that they were in trouble a typical line of questioning would go very much like this:-

Defence: "Officer when you searched my clients person you say you found a substance that you later found to be cannabis. Is that correct?"

Officer: "Yes that is correct."

Defence: "What made you assume it was cannabis when you found it?"

Officer: "I asked him what it was and he said it was weed, which is slang for cannabis. And later I carried out a field test which proved positive, and the Government Chemist tested along with the other substances and they all proved positive."

Defence: "Are you sure my client admitted to knowing it cannabis at the time of its discovery?"

Officer: "Yes I am."

Defence; "Would it surprise you Officer to learn that my client states quite categorically that he didn't tell you it was cannabis?"

The Officer, not knowing if that is a question that requires an answer or is the Defending Counsel just showboating, looks at the Prosecuting Counsel and the Judge.

Judge: "Mr Smith"; the Defending Counsel; "are you expecting an answer or simply making a point?"

Defence: "I would like an answer m'lud."

Judge: "Officer please answer the question."

Now at this point the officer would like to say. "No, nothing this devious little toe rag says could surprise me". But he realises that although this would make him personally feel a whole lot better, it wouldn't go down well with the Jury and would probably attract a reprimand from the Judge. So instead he says:-

Officer: "Yes it would surprise me."

Defence: "Well I can assure you Officer he is quite adamant he never mentioned the words cannabis or weed. And no I don't expect an answer to that. However I would like you tell the Court which pocket you allege the cannabis was found in."

At this point the Prosecuting Counsel objects to the word allege. The objection is sustained as at no stage has it been denied cannabis was found in one of the defendants pockets.

Defence: "Then I'll rephrase the question. In which pocket did you find the cannabis?"

Officer: "The right hand pocket of his jacket."

Defence: "The right hand pocket?"

Officer: "Yes, the right hand pocket of his jacket."

Defence: "Not the left hand pocket?"

The Officer makes a show of looking back at his Official Notebook.

Officer: "No the right hand pocket."

Defence: "Are you sure, only my client informs me it was in the left hand pocket, not as you claim the right hand pocket?"

Officer: "No it was definitely the right hand pocket."

Defence; "How can you be so sure? It's easy to mix up right and left in stressful situations like this, and one's memory can play tricks."

At this point the Officer is again tempted say. "What bloody difference does it make which pocket it was in if he admits it was in one of them?" However he doesn't. He realises the Defence is trying to cast doubts on the accuracy of his evidence. So he explains that there were two Officers involved with the SOP, one of whom was writing down exactly what was happening as it happened so there was no chance a mistake was made. The fact that the Defendant was carrying some cannabis is not in question. There is obviously something coming up later that will be much more pertinent to the guilt or otherwise of his client and the Defence are trying to make the Officer look inefficient and unsure in the eyes of the Jury. This is no more than a bit of gentle cat and mouse, however on occasion it can get very nasty.

**

An Officer who was known to all and sundry by his nickname Chak, and who we have seen previously, was on duty in the Green Channel in Terminal Two. He was watching the passengers off of the Lufthansa 6404 from Frankfurt as they filed through the Green. Chak was particularly interested in this flight as it connected with a flight from Lagos in Nigeria. Lagos was a high risk point of departure for almost every kind of drugs. Heroin, Cocaine, cannabis; they all came here from Lagos. What made this type of flight particularly attractive to the drug smuggler was the fact that it wasn't direct from a high risk airport. They knew that we watched the direct flights very closely, but didn't have the resources to cover every flight. So if they could appear to be arriving from somewhere deemed low risk, such as Frankfurt, it increased their chances of getting through unscathed.

Chak was stopping as many passengers as he could, as he was showing a new boy, Barry, the ropes. He had just finished with a passenger when he noticed a young unusually smart Nigerian man (he was only eighteen and it later turned out he was a Public School boy} walking through the Green. Chak stopped him and went through the normal questions.

The young man, Victor Enahoro, was carrying a hard sided Samsonite suitcase. As soon as Chak opened it Enahoro denied it was his. Chak checked the baggage tag on suitcase against the tag on the ticket. Surprise, surprise, the tag on the ticket was missing. There were signs however that there had been a tag but it had been torn off. Now who would tear of a baggage tag from their ticket unless they had something to hide? Subsequently it would be proved by Scotland Yard's forensic department that there were traces of the glue used by airlines to attach tags to tickets, on the ticket. There was no shaving equipment, razor, or shoes in the suitcase. In fact there was nothing in there to prove it belonged to Enahoro. There was however, 2.5 kilos of cannabis, which although it was only a relatively small amount, was enough to put Enahoro in front of a Judge and Jury.

Enahoro, who was the son of a former Nigerian Oil Minister, continued to deny ownership of the suitcase. Chak knew this wasn't going to be easy. Most importantly, as it later transpired, Enahoro denied ever using or even knowing about cannabis. An amazing assertion from a person coming from somewhere that was at the time one of the cannabis capitals of the world.

With the lack of admissions and the lack of a baggage tag there was a long discussion between Chak and the various Senior Officers on duty as to whether or not Enahoro should be charged.

Was it just a coincidence that Enahoro had picked up someone else's suitcase? Was it a coincidence that the baggage tag was missing from the ticket? Was it a coincidence that there was no corresponding matching suitcase still going round and round on the baggage carousel? Was it a coincidence that this must mean another passenger, the smuggler, had made the same mistake as Enahoro? Was it also a coincidence that Enahoro was the only Nigerian out of a population of over 100 million who had never heard of cannabis and didn't know it was illegal to import into the United Kingdom? This was a Public School student Chak was dealing with, there was no way he didn't know this.

Eventually an SO, let's call him Ken, a determined, tough Scot, who took no nonsense from anyone, and certainly didn't believe a word Enahoro said; listened to Chaks vehement assertions regarding Enahoros involvement, and took the decision to charge him. So Enahoro was charged with being knowingly concerned in the attempted fraudulent evasion of the prohibition, contrary to Section 170 (2) of the Customs and Excise Management Act 1979, and Section 3 of the Misuse of Drugs Act 1971. He was duly deposited in the Heathrow nick waiting to be taken to Uxbridge Magistrates Court, where hopefully he would be remanded in custody and eventually be committed to Crown Court for trial.

Next day, Chak and Mike a member of the Customs Investigation Unit (CIU), were preparing the Property List for court. The suitcase had been removed from the Terminal Two Lock-up and they were busy itemising the contents. Among other things there was a suit, a T-shirt, and a blue denim waistcoat. As Mike took the waistcoat out of the suitcase and was about to hand it to Chak he felt something in the pen pocket. As he drew it out at first he thought was in fact a pen. Then he realised that what he was holding was cannabis joint, a spliff.

Now the positive aspect of finding this joint was that as long as the jury were convinced of the fact that the suitcase did belong to Enahoro, then his assertions about knowing nothing about cannabis were obviously lies. They, the jury, would then be very likely to conclude that the lies were an attempt to convince them that the cannabis wasn't his. The down side was that it would be very difficult to present to the Court. The Defence would certainly accuse Mike and Chak of planting the joint in the waistcoat. The Solicitor's Office were even considering dropping the case completely. Chaks position was very precarious and one SO, we'll call him Pete, even suggested he should be suspended while it was investigated. Not only did this not happen, but an Assistant Collector who we will call Ron, fully supported Chak and persuaded the Collector to add his support. With all this support the Solicitors Office decided to press on with the charge. Chak added a supplementary Witness Statement detailing exactly what had happened and this was attached to his original Statement.

The trial opened at Reading Crown Court on 6th September 1979. It was a momentous day for Chak earlier that morning his wife had presented him with a bonny baby girl. It was his first child and he was on cloud nine.

Later his interrogation by the Defending Counsel, Mr Julian Milne, would bring him down off of that cloud with a resounding bump.

The Court was sitting before His Honour Judge John Murchie. His Honour was veteran of many Customs trials and would become famous on the circuit as one of the fairest Judges, and one of those with the most common sense. Also he showed an intense dislike for drug smugglers, he demonstrated this as reported previously, when he sentenced Montereaux to twelve years in Strangeways. Chak was obviously the star of the show. The whole case hinged around his evidence. In this situation there is only one thing the Officer can do and that is tell the truth and be open about the error that had been made. But there was no doubt Mr Milne, the Defending Counsel, wasn't going to let him off that easy. Time after time he attacked Chak over the "magical discovery of a cannabis joint in the waistcoat pocket some thirty hours after the initial interception". Of course as stated earlier, if he had found it at the time, the "knowingly concerned" part of the charge would have been proved beyond doubt. Mr Milne continued his relentless attack. At one time it was so ferocious that Judge Murchie instructed the Court Usher to provide Chak with a drink of water. And remember this was a day when Chak had become a father at six in the morning. He had been up all night waiting for the arrival of his baby daughter. And Chak really wasn't a morning type of person.

Mr Milne's accusation was that between the time of the arrest and the discovery of the joint, Chak had ample time to enter the Terminal Two Lock Up, where the cannabis and the property were detained, break the seal on the exhibit bag, plant the cannabis joint in the waistcoat pocket, reseal the exhibit bag, and wait for it to be discovered when the Property List was prepared by the CIU. And by so doing prove Enharo's guilt. Simple common sense members of the jury.

It was looking bad, the members of the Jury seemed to be believing what they were hearing from the Defending Counsel. Chak could see the odd wry smile and the sideways glances. No doubt about it Chak was under pressure. He was also running backwards and forwards to the Royal

Berkshire Hospital to see mum and baby in the Maternity Ward. At times like this it's very often a case of how you answer questions not the actual answer. That's always going to be the truth, but how you phrase your answer and the emphasis you put on certain words or phrases can make all the difference between a Jury believing you, or not.

By the third day Chak was still under attack and a lot of Officers might have buckled under that pressure. But Chak, who had studied at Oxford, and who had a masterful command of the English language, even though he originated from the Sub-Continent, was made of sterner stuff. On that third day in response to yet another onslaught the Officer made the following statement:-

Chak: "Sir you are quite right to accuse me of planting this cannabis cigarette in your client's clothing, which he had claimed wasn't his."

You can imagine the looks on the Jurors faces when Chak said this. But he went on:-

"That said, the Terminal Lock Up is so closely guarded and supervised by other Customs staff and the supervising Senior Officers, that I needed to be Harry Houdini in order to enter into it, break the seal, plant the offending evidence, re-seal the suitcase and come out without being seen. Sir, life in HM Customs just isn't like that."

Milne: But Officer I am simply redrawing the facts, which you consistently deny. Do you not see that the facts, as I attempted to lay them out, show palpable doubt in your credibility before the Court?"

Chak: "No Sir. You might consider your assumed story to be facts. But they are a farrago of twisted facts, which need to be judged on their own merit."

Chak had taken a real gamble in challenging the Defending Counsel in such a manner. Later events would prove his gamble worked. At the time the

Court went completely silent. Everybody looked at one another. Nobody had a clue what a farrago was. There was an unconfirmed rumour that the Jury requested that the Usher bring a copy of the Oxford Concise Dictionary to the Jury Room, so they could look it up.

The case concluded with the Jury finding Enahoro guilty, so as stated previously Chaks gamble paid off. Before he sentenced Enahoro to three years at Her Majesty's Pleasure, Judge Murchie called Chak back into the Witness Box. This is word for word what he said.

"It was a difficult case for the Prosecution in the light of the Defence strategy. However, this court would like to acknowledge the Officers composure under severe pressure, his knowledge of the law and his command on the English language. I found it particularly impressive that, despite the stress caused by such a serious allegation, of planting evidence, against an officer of Her Majesty's Customs, the witness provided all his answers in a cohesive manner and even using a saying used by a former British Prime Minister in order to sustain his stance of probity. I would like the court to convey this commendation to Her Majesty's Commissioners, saying that it must have been one of the finest examples of prosecution evidence given in court under challenging circumstances."

Praise indeed for Chak. And he never let his mates forget it.

**

John a wiry, determined, ultra-professional, Officer, was on duty in the Green Channel, Terminal Four, watching the passengers from the BA078 from Accra as they made their way through the Channel. It was often said of John that in a previous life he must have been a woman. Not because he was at all effeminate, but because he was never wrong and always had to have the last word. And on this occasion against all the odds he most certainly did.

He noticed a woman who fitted the profile of a West African swallower. This woman was Helen Ladiende. Ms Ladiende lived in Accra she was just visiting for a few days. She didn't know where she was staying, she was going to find somewhere now she was here. She had very little money with her, certainly not enough to pay for a room for the week she said she was staying. She had no credit cards. This wasn't looking good for Helen, then it got worse. Her ticket was cash paid and was open ended, that is there was no return date. It was looking worse and worse. Open ended tickets were common with swallowers. They would go back as soon as the last package had been retrieved, and the digestive system being what it is, you could never be sure when that would be. On top of that of course if the packages unravelled they might not need a return ticket at all. John asked her to put her suitcase on the bench. It was only small, typical baggage for a swallower. It didn't have a baggage label so almost certainly it had fitted in the overhead locker. Swallowers often only had carry-on baggage yet for some reason they always came through with the bulk of the passengers who had checked-in baggage. Perhaps they thought they wouldn't be noticed in the crowd!!

John had just started searching her baggage when he noticed a passenger who had stopped on the other side of the Green Channel had opened his suitcase and appeared to be looking for something inside it. Whatever he was looking for he couldn't find it. Perhaps he couldn't find it because he was spending most of his time trying to see what was happening with Helen Ladiende. John left Ladiende standing at the bench while he went and spoke to the man opposite. This person was bizarrely named "Innocent" Garland. John felt sure he was connected to Ladiende. A quick check showed that he also had a cash paid open ended ticket. He thought he was probably her "minder".

At this point John had no hard evidence against either of them, but John being John: and you could never accuse him of negativity; he arrested then both and marched them off to adjoining Interview Rooms. Once they were in the Interview Rooms he had Ladiende searched by female officers, and he and another male officer searched Garland. At this point he had a massive piece of luck. In the left hand pocket of Garlands' jacket he found the torn off neck of a blue balloon.

"Is that important?" I hear you say.

"Too right it is", says John.

But why is it important. Well, John now thinks he has the missing link between Ladiende and Garland. John is convinced Ladiende is a swallower. By this time an EMIT test has been carried out and she is positive for heroin. At the time the most popular way of packaging drugs for swallowing them was to simply put them in balloons and tie the neck. Much as you would do if you were blowing up balloons to decorate your house for a party. John was convinced that this piece of balloon had been broken off when Garland was filling the balloons that were in Ladiendes stomach. He fully expected that when Ladiende produced her lethal load he would find balloons to match the piece he had obtained from Garland's pocket. Not the actual one, but made of the same type of rubber. He hoped forensic tests would be able to prove the link.

At this point fortunately for John he showed the piece of balloon to several Officers and the Senior Officer on duty. Let's call the SO Jim. I say fortunately because at this point John's already tenuous connection between Ladiende and Garland took a bit of a knock.

There was big job going down and a lot of Customs Investigation types were around wanting to interview some not very nice people who were connected to another very very not nice person by the name of Curtis Warren. He, Curtis Warren, is by the way, currently serving a long stretch in HMP Full Sutton, near York, for conspiracy to smuggle cannabis into Jersey. And he is famous, or notorious, for being the only known drug smuggler to appear in the Times Rich List, his fortune valued by the Times in 1998 at £40 million.

Anyway, John was asked, by Jim, to vacate his two Interview Rooms and re-locate to two other rooms. At the same time the Officer named Malc who we met earlier with the plantains, was also being asked to vacate his room for the same reason. Just before they moved John showed Malc the piece of blue balloon and explained to George where it had come from.

It was chaos moving the three potential smugglers. It was a tight little corridor, it was secluded, and close to the Custody office, which is why the Investigators wanted to use it. All the baggage had to be moved, all the evidence had to be bagged up and moved, the prisoners had to be moved, all the paper work had to be carefully gathered up and moved. It wasn't helped by the fact that Malc's prisoner was schizophrenic and he was extremely distressed at having to move. At one point he refused to budge, he had got used to this office and he quite liked it. He was confused and was having trouble deciding what was reality, and what wasn't. So this sudden upheaval only made him worse. He was definitely ill but as he was carrying half a kilo of cannabis Malc had enough grounds to be holding him.

John had put the piece of blue balloon in his Notebook - there were no little plastic bags for evidence in those days, and his Notebook was on the desk with the rest of the paperwork. Eventually all three prisoners were deposited into their new homes and all the baggage was moved and everything started to settle down again. John got himself ready to interview Garland. He opened his Notebook and realised that the piece of blue balloon, his only piece of real evidence, was gone. He searched everywhere. Went back to the room that he'd been in previously, searched the corridors, and re-searched the baggage. He had Garland strip searched again just in case he'd managed to lift it during the changeover. It was definitely gone. Had Garland swallowed it? John didn't think so, but nevertheless Garland was put on the Frost machine for the next few days. Nothing came out except a rather long reptile that looked like a cross between an earthworm and grass snake. What happened to the piece of blue balloon was never established. Maybe Garland had swallowed it and the worm snake had then swallowed it. Customs didn't have any way of checking faeces of the reptile.

John completed his investigation as best he could. Ladiende eventually produced over three-hundred balloons containing slightly over half a kilo of heroin. Garland was held until John was happy he had nothing incriminating in his stomach. The worm or snake or whatever it was, was interesting but didn't actually prove anything. John, after taking advice from the HM Customs and Excise Solicitors Office, charged them both with conspiracy to import heroin. This was amazing. The Sol's Office had never been known for taking brave decisions. But on this occasion they decided to run with it. It obviously wasn't an issue with Ladiende, however the evidence against Garland was all circumstantial except for the piece of blue balloon, which was now missing.

The two of them duly appeared in Magistrates Court and again amazingly they were both eventually committed to stand trial at Crown Court. After prisoners are charged this is the first real test of the evidence. Because of the amount of drugs involved, the Magistrates aren't looking to find them guilty or not guilty they are just looking to see if there is enough evidence to warrant the case going to a higher court where appropriate sentences can be handed out if they are found guilty. They decided there was. Amazing!

By this time at least six Officers had put in Witness Statements stating that on such and such day at a certain time John Parsons had shown them a piece of blue balloon that he had found in Innocent Garland's left hand pocket. All the Officers who had given Witness Statements were called to Isleworth Crown Court as witnesses. The Defence had indicated that they would not just accept the Statements. They would want to cross examine the Officers. So of course they had to be there.

It could have started better for HM Customs. When it got to the blue balloon the first witness called was the SO, Jim. Jim got up and gave his evidence. The Defence moved in. He poured scorn on Jim's version of events. Maybe it was because he was the first witness re the blue balloon. Maybe it was because he wasn't in uniform like all the rest of the Officers, and the Defence thought he might not be as professional as they thought the Officers would be. Whatever the reason, he gave Jim hell. Jim stood his ground but when the Defence barrister accused him of lying he couldn't take any more.

"I assure you I do not lie. I am a Roman Catholic." Said Jim.

"Yes but so indeed are most of the IRA." Replied the Defending Counsel with a huge grin on his face.

Jim looked most abashed. The Court dissolved into fits of laughter.

Not a good start.

"Order, order", says the Judge. But even he has a bit of a twinkle in his eye.

It was an important lesson. Never say more than you have to. Never show you're being rattled. Just answer the question and let the Jury decide. You never win in a war of words with the legal boys. They're too smart by half. Anyway, next came Malc. The cross examination was a little strenuous but nothing like Jim's. Then the rest one after another.

"I was on duty on the such and such date when John showed me a piece of blue balloon etc etc."

After the sixth or seventh Officer, the Defending Counsel did an astonishing thing. Almost as if he was making his closing speech, he turned to the jury, and virtually accused the Officers and Jim of entering into a conspiracy with John.

"Isn't amazing how everybody who was on duty on such and such date saw this mythical piece of blue balloon?" Conspiracy!!!!

Up jumped the Prosecuting Counsel.

"Objection, Your Honour."

"Sustained," said the Judge.

The jury are instructed to ignore the Defending Counsel's remarks.

Malc was sent post haste back to Terminal Four. The trial was nearing its conclusion. His instruction was to grab anybody who had been on duty on that day and who hadn't seen the blue balloon. He rounded up six or seven officers who were on duty on the day and dragged them off to Isleworth. They quickly prepared Witness Statements and were put in the Witness Box by the Prosecution.

So having had a succession of officers getting into the Witness Box stating they'd seen the piece of blue balloon. We now had a whole succession of witnesses standing up and saying they'd been on duty and they hadn't seen the piece of blue balloon. One even stated that not only had he not seen the piece of blue balloon he hadn't even seen John or Jim. It really had all the elements of a Brian Rix farce. Eventually the Judge called halt to the procession of officers and the trial proceeded.

The outcome of this incredible series of events, was that the Jury found them both guilty. You just cannot tell how a case like this will go. Undoubtedly the Defence's decision to dispute the very existence of the blue balloon, had planted the thought in the minds of the Jury that if they believed there was a piece of balloon then Garland was guilty. If they didn't believe there was, then he was innocent. Fortunately for John they obviously believed there was. This victory was especially pleasing for the Prosecuting Counsel as he came from a lower Panel than his adversary, the Defending Counsel. So in football terms it was a bit like a Championship side knocking a Premiership team out of the FA Cup. John of course was delighted. He really did like to have the last word.

**

Criminal attempts

In the war on drugs nothing was ever as it seemed, you couldn't believe the evidence of your own eyes. Everybody was out to fool everybody else. The officer stops a man who ticks all the boxes. He must be up to something. But he isn't, there's nothing there. An officer in the Red Channel has a passenger in front of him who on the face of it appears to be an honest upright citizen declaring his excess goods. But the officer is new and is looking at everybody. He finds five kilos of heroin.

A man from Dacca in Bangladesh is pushing three trolleys with a suite of bedroom furniture on them. He must have something there. Why bring over a suite of bedroom furniture that is rubbish. He must have something there. But he hasn't. He has brought it over because an aunt has left it to him in her will and he doesn't want to offend the family. The furniture is examined to the point where it can no longer be put back together again. There's nothing there. Still at least he's only got one trolley to push now, and he does get compensated for his loss.

A couple are acting so calm they must be up to something. They are, they have pinched the dressing gowns from their Hilton Hotel room, and they are determined not to act nervous or guilty.

This man in the Red Channel declares a kitchen sink. Surely this can't be real. People don't buy kitchen sinks on a trip abroad. Maybe it's merchandise. Maybe there is something concealed within it. But no, it is a kitchen sink, in fact it's his wife's birthday present! Amazing, who said romance is dead. He was advised to have a first aid kit handy when he gave it to her.

Nothing is what it seems. Everybody is trying to fool everybody. The smuggler is trying to fool the Customs Officers and the Officers are trying to kid the smugglers. We want them to think that we're ahead of the game, that we're much more professional than we really are. However this mutual deception is to be expected. What we don't expect is the villain trying to fool the villain, and this does happen.

**

Norman or Norm as he was known to his colleagues was an easy going sort of Officer. He was a medium sort of guy. Liked a drink, but not too much. Supported Charlton Athletic but didn't get over excited about them. Got on well with his team but didn't have any close friends. Could be a bit moody but was never bad tempered. He was an easy going medium sort of chap, just like a lot of the offices we've met in this book.

As he stood watching the RG – Aerolineas Argentinas - from Buenos Aires come though the Green in Terminal Four, he wasn't ever so interested. He was coming to the end of a long stretch without a day off and he was looking forward to some time at home. His SO, Let's call him Mike, was also looking forward to his time off. "Come on Norm", he said, "show the rest of this lot how it's done". Not very subtle but then Mike was about as subtle as hippopotamus. It was his last remark before he disappeared into the Smoking Room. It was obviously meant to be motivational.

It did however spur Norm into action. Perhaps spur is a bit strong, Norm was never animated enough to be spurred, but it did move him into action. He watched Mike shuffle off to the smoking room and started to look a little more closely at the passengers streaming through. The main mass of the passengers had gone through but it hadn't quite reached the straggler stage so there was still a fair choice.

He stopped a South American looking woman and then as he was talking to her he noticed a man pushing a trolley with two hard sided suitcases on it. He didn't fit. He didn't look right for the RG from BA. He looked more like someone who had been out to Brussels or Paris for a day working. An engineer or something like that. Or maybe he was on his way to do the weekend shopping. He just didn't look right for the Buenos Aries flight. He obviously wasn't a business man, he didn't look South American, of any nationality. He didn't look like holiday maker either from or to Argentina, he didn't look like he had enough money to just jet about for the sheer hell of it, he obviously wasn't a polo player, no horse. He definitely didn't fit. But on the other hand he was travelling alone, and he was pushing two hard sided suitcases.

Norm stopped him in his usual understated way.

"Hello sir, just bring your trolley over here for a moment could you?"

Ever so polite and relaxed was Norm. The passenger was a resident of this country, he lived in Birmingham, he'd been away for ten days, and he was returning from Buenos Aries, where, as he put it, he'd been for a bit of a break. Frederick Phillipson was too relaxed. He had paid for his ticket using a credit card at a Thomas Cook's in Sparkhill, a suburb of Birmingham. As he said, he'd been away for ten days. Doing not a lot. The Touristers, that is the suitcases, looked very new.

"What did you do for ten days?" asked Norm.

"Not a lot really, went to some clubs, had look round the city. Just hung out really. Fancied a break and it seemed like an interesting place to go to".

"First time abroad?" Asked Norm?

"No I've been to Majorca on holiday"

Now this didn't add up. If someone who's only ever been to Majorca decides to have a break somewhere interesting why would they go to Buenos Aires. Why not Paris, Rome, Barcelona, somewhere a lot closer, and a lot cheaper to get to. Especially as further questioning revealed that he was unemployed and currently of no fixed abode.

"Are the suitcases new?"

"Yes the old ones were damaged on the way out".

"Did you pack them?"

"Course."

"Are you carrying any packages for anyone?"

"No, not likely."

"What makes you say it like that?"

"Well you never know what you might be stitched up with."

"Do you mean drugs?"

"Yes drugs, or anything else."

This was good for Norm because he had now established knowledge of the prohibition.

"Have you got a receipt for the suitcases?"

"I might have somewhere, but they were only cheap."

By this time Norm knew that Frederick Phillipson was up to something, he just wasn't sure what. He didn't fit the usual photo-fit of a mule. Argentina wasn't a regular route for cocaine but it did happen. Anywhere in South America was easy to access from Colombia and Bolivia so they were high risk, just not as high. On top of that there was always the chance that it might be uncut emeralds or diamonds. But the suitcases were definitely pointing towards coke, or Charlie as they were calling it at that particular time.

Apart from the suitcases, Phillipson only had a bottle and a carton to declare. Phillipson lifted the first case onto the bench. It seemed quite heavy from what Norm could see, but strangely when he opened it, it didn't have much in the way of clothing or anything else. Why did he need two suitcases? There was nothing of interest in the first suitcase, but as Norm moved it around on the bench it felt heavier than it should have and it didn't seem quite balanced. Then he had a look at the second case and sure enough it was exactly the same. Norm knew he was dealing with a double sided or top and bottomed concealment.

This was all straight forward, nothing too unusual. Eventually each suitcase would prove to have 4.6 kilos of a white powdery substance that gave a positive reaction to the cocaine field test. It wasn't possible to run it. Mike the SO didn't have enough staff to be able to carry out a run safely, and there were no Enforcement or Investigation Teams around. So Phillipson was marched off into an interview room, the drugs were revealed. Shock horror of course from Mr Phillipson, how did they get there, he wanted to know?

Eventually he calmed down. He was interviewed on tape with a Solicitor present. He was an amateur. After some, actually a lot, of painstaking questioning, including demonstrations of how obvious the extra weight was. Phillipson admitted he knew it was there. It was unusual in as much as he admitted everything. He was a Lone Ranger, operating alone. He had been made redundant so he was desperate for money. He'd seen cocaine being pushed in the local pubs and clubs in Birmingham, especially in the Bull Ring area, he knew how much it went for. So quite simply he had gone to BA on a fishing expedition. He scraped together every penny he could. He had his redundancy money, he moved out of his flat, got his deposit back, he even sold his car and the furniture from his flat.

He bought himself a return ticket to Argentina, flew out, checked into a small cheap hotel, went round the clubs until he was approached with some Charlie, and bingo he had made his contact. He found he had enough money to buy 9.2 kilos of cocaine concealed in the false back of two suitcases. This all shows just what an amateur he was. If he'd flown to Jamaica the flight and the Charlie would have been cheaper. He would probably have been able to buy another two or three kilos.

This was all straightforward. He was charged and the cocaine was sent to the Government Chemist near Waterloo in London for analysis. Norm was chuffed, so was Mike his SO. Norm had been working hard but he hadn't had a sniff for a couple of months. This wasn't unusual, officers could and often did go months without any success. Finding drug smugglers was hard and often tedious work.

Anyway back to Norm and Mr Phillipson. He was incarcerated in Wormwood Scrubs waiting for his day in court. Norm was getting on with his Witness Statement and all the other paperwork that needed to be done. He was busy in General Office working away on the case when the Duty SO strolled into the room and told Norm that the Government Chemist was on the telephone in the SO's office. Now this was strange. The Gov Chem normally just sent a report confirming the drug, giving a weight and the purity. This was then presented in court and that was the end of his involvement. Norm had never had one ring him up. He just couldn't believe what he had heard. Whatever it was that Phillipson had imported, it wasn't cocaine. In fact it wasn't a prohibited substance at all. It did contain something that contained a blue whitener, something like soap powder. Which was why it had given a positive reaction to the cocaine field test.

As stated previously Norm was a middle of the road sort of chap so he didn't panic, but he was extremely concerned. Phillipson had been charged with an offence that he hadn't committed. He needn't have worried, the Solicitors Office simply removed the original Charge and replaced it with another relating to the Criminal Attempts Act 1981 Para 1 (1). The fact that it was impossible for him to commit the original offence because the substance wasn't cocaine was covered by sub section 2. This states quite clearly that an offender can be guilty even if the facts make committing the offence impossible.

Norm had the pleasure of interviewing Phillipson again in the Scrubs. He removed one charge and replaced it with another. For a moment Phillipson was elated, but this didn't last long when his Solicitor told him that the amount of time he could be given was exactly the same as with the previous charge.

So what had happened? Quite simply the bad guys out in Buenos Aries realised Phillipson was a Lone Ranger and that he wasn't connected to any organisations. So they ripped him off. They had added something like a washing powder with a blue whitener in it. This would make the powder turn blue. They did this just in case Phillipson had a means of testing the "coke" before he handed over the money. Norm didn't think there was the remotest chance he would have tested it.

Phillipson duly appeared at Isleworth Crown Court and received a sentence of six years. This was a little bit on the low side so perhaps the Judge did take a little pity on him. Between them the dealers and Norm had done Phillipson a huge favour. If he had started selling the-would be cocaine around the pubs and clubs in Birmingham then his clients would not have been very happy and somebody would have knifed him. But even if it had been the real thing, the Asian gangs that operated mainly out of the Sparkhill district in Birmingham, which coincidentally was where Phillipson had lived, wouldn't have been very happy either. In all probability they would have kneecapped him. Norm did try to explain to him what a favour he'd done him, and how lucky he was he'd been caught, he just didn't appear to appreciate it at the time.

**

$$\textbf{4}$$

Getting Professional

Alpha One

By the early 1990's it was obvious things had to change. With ever reducing resources and the increased professionalism of the smuggling cartels HM Customs just couldn't keep up. So what do the Civil Service do when they need to solve a problem? Yes, that's right, they had a Review.

The Review of Anti-Smuggling Controls (RASC) 1992, was intended to be the vehicle that would put HM Customs into the right shape to properly fight the drug smuggler. The Review itself would in fact have solved many of the problems that Customs struggled with. Sadly it was left to individual Collections or Regions to interpret or adapt the Review to match their local needs. The most obvious change at Heathrow was that a sizeable minority of officers were removed from Green Channel duties and they took control of the Red Channels, the Outward Control Posts, the Lock-Ups and everything else that in theory didn't actually involve catching smugglers. They formed the Passenger Services Division (PSD) and those catching the smugglers formed the Anti-Smuggling Division (ASD). This already ridiculous situation was made worse when PSD officers in the Red Channel were instructed not to look in suitcases. In fact they were not only told not to look in suitcases, they were told they would be disciplined if they did. It was as if some of the people implementing the Review had lost touch with reality and had assumed that smugglers wouldn't use the Red Channel. Or maybe they thought the smugglers would play by the rules and restrict their efforts to the Green. As you will have read previously this was palpably not the case. The Red Channel was and will always be a source of high quality drug seizures. There will always be the drug smuggler who thinks the double bluff of using the Red is worth the risk. This situation reached its ridiculous height when a Terminal Three Senior Officer, who might have been called Gordon, was threatened with disciplinary action. Gordon responded by issuing his own threats intending to sue his managers if he was prevented from carrying out his duties in the proper manner. He did say he would take it to the House of Lords if necessary.

The lunacy of the situation was encapsulated when the then Assistant Collector declared that his new Anti-Smuggling Division would be the most highly trained Division in the UK. In the same breath he announced that no Anti-Smuggling officers would be allowed to act as trainers. He never explained who would deliver the training his highly trained officers would receive. The only people who really knew about catching drug smugglers were the officers in his Division.

This crazy situation was allowed to remain in place until 1995 when, following a change in Senior Management, two Assistant Collectors who we will call Geoff and Derek, used some common sense and this particular directive was removed. Now common sense isn't a quality normally associated with senior managers but these two must have been the exception that proves the rule. Officers in the Red were again free to do their job properly. However the partition remained. Despite this change the officers of PSD were gradually more and more de-skilled in finding and dealing with drugs. They continued to make seizures of revenue goods. Cameras, jewellery, fur coats, cigarettes, or spirits, were fine. But if they felt they had a drug suspect they were expected to inform an Anti-Smuggling team and hand the passenger to them to progress. This was simply doomed to failure. The PSD officers didn't want to hand over seizures and the AS officers didn't want to take over jobs that weren't theirs and for which they would get little credit.

Eventually in 2003, the Collector at the time, Mike, acting on an initiative from the then Chairman of the Board, Sir Richard Broadbent, put into motion the de-RASCing of Heathrow. The PSD and ASD Divisions merged to become Detection Divisions. The idea being that now all officers would cover the full range of duties. As it was pre RASC there would be officers who were more comfortable doing one part of the job and others who preferred something different, but they would all be trained and skilled to do everything.

RASC did however bring with it many benefits, and results did improve. The officers of ASD became more skilled and experienced because they weren't spending time in the other areas carrying out non drug related duties. The National training improved, although the local training team was removed. The latter did eventually return as a much more effective unit with the power to refuse trainees who didn't make the mark. The main improvement that came out of RASC was the introduction of the Control Surveyor, or Alpha One; that was their radio call sign; as he or she was universally known. The name survived until some faceless bureaucrat, who we'll call Stuart, decided that this title was too emotive and changed it to Control Surveyor. But to the officers they remained as Alpha One, and it was the officers who mattered.

Prior to RASC, the individual teams, and Districts, operated in isolation with their own objectives and targets. You would often have different Team Leaders fighting over the same piece of information. Teams turning up for the same high-risk flight leaving other flights to go through without a Customs Officer in sight. With the introduction of Alpha One this all changed. Like the Fat Controller in the Tommy the Tank Engine books, Alpha One controlled the whole of Heathrow or whichever theatre of operations they were based in. They knew how many Baggage officers they had in the Terminals, how many Tarmac officers they had working on the Tarmac, how many Rummage Crews, Dog Teams, Freight Teams, Detection Information Teams (DITs), how many Custody Officers and the number of prisoners they were guarding. They also knew how many high risk flights, from places such as Bogota, Lagos, Kingston, Islamabad, Bangkok, would land on their shift. They would have information from Drugs Liaison Officers (DLOs) based abroad in places such as those just mentioned. Alpha One would also have information from the Police, the Security Services, and the public. Alpha One enabled Customs to focus officers where they were most needed. He, or she, would look at the information, look at the risk flights, prioritise, and then deploy resources accordingly.

They started each shift with a type of balance sheet in front of them. On the one side of the balance sheet, let's call it the debit side were the lists of high risk flights during the watch. Then there was the information from the DLO's, the Police, MI5, MI6, the public. That was the "to do" list. Then on the other side, the credit side. How many teams, and how many people on each team in the Terminals. How many teams how many officers on the Tarmac area. Looking on aeroplanes, looking at bags before they came into the Reclaim Hall. Checking the Transit sheds. Keeping their eyes peeled for things that didn't look right. For instance, why was there an Air Canada van on the Stands used by British Airways? What were they up to? How many Dog teams available. How many people on that little team called the DITs; the Detection Information Teams. Checking lists of suspects against the passenger lists of incoming and outgoing flights. Looking at strange flight patterns. Wondering why Mr Smith of London is flying direct to Bogota but on his return journey has decided to come via Paris. Could be quite innocent, but it could be something darker. Does he know we'll be watching the Bogota, but thinks we won't be watching the Paris? The DITs and the Dogs were the great imponderables, you never knew just what they would come up with. So how many DIT Officers and who they were was very important.

It was the responsibility of Alpha One to make sure that all those risks on the Debit side of the Balance Sheet were covered by the resources on the Credit side. No teams were just left to their own devices. They would have their own plans and targets which they would pursue when not needed by Alpha One, but they would be controlled by Alpha One. The improvement in operations cannot be over emphasised.

The Alpha One job was on the one hand the most rewarding exciting job in HM Customs but on the other it was always the most stressful. Whatever happened during the watch it was the responsibility of Alpha One. If there were prisoners at risk, that is those with internal concealments, he was responsible for their health and safety. As has been said previously in one year there were three deaths in custody, two at Heathrow and one at Gatwick. If a run was being organised it was up to Alpha One; this would eventually be the sole responsibility of the Senior Investigation Officer, the SIO; to make sure there were enough plain clothes officers available, it was his decision. If it went wrong he would be held to account.

Every decision that wasn't in the rule book was his or hers. The body of a known drug gang member was being flown home from Accra. The information Alpha One had told him that the man's gang in Brixton were very excited about it and were in a party mood. Alpha One's first decision. Do we open up the coffin? After the coffin is opened and nothing is found does he investigate a possible internal concealment? The man has died from falling off of a motorbike. But had he already swallowed packages? Was that perhaps why he fell off of his motorbike? So it's down to Alpha One. Does he have the cadaver opened or maybe x-rayed? Would Hillingdon Hospital be prepared to x-ray a corpse? Does he instruct a team to carry this onerous task or does he seek volunteers? It's Sunday morning and he's the man in charge. There's nobody, not even on the end of a telephone, to ask. There's nothing in the Customs Codes to cover this situation. At this point it comes down to experience and common sense. If there aren't drugs involved why is everybody back in Brixton so excited? A Senior Officer called Bob volunteered himself and two of his team to check the body out. They accompanied it to the funeral parlour. Inspected the body with a doctor. Cause of death needed to be established so a post mortem was carried out with Customs in attendance. No drugs! But the decision that Alpha One had to make was typical of their role.

**

You have read previously about Leroy Winston Montereaux, a violent Yardie from Manchester (See Chapter 3 "The JM001 and the BA262"). This case was typical of the difficult stressful decisions that had to be made by Alpha One or their equivalent prior to RASC. Wally had stopped Leroy and had established that he was carrying suitcases with false sides. He didn't know what was in them but he was sure it would be drugs. Why else would a person go to the trouble of having a suitcase specially made with a double skin? Sometimes the excuse would be, "I thought I was carrying diamonds or emeralds", or some other less serious commodity.

But in reality, no Customs Officer had ever seen a false sided suitcase containing anything but drugs. Although the previously mentioned Malcolm (Chapter 3 "Concealments become more devious") did once stumble across a Nigerian gentleman importing money in the false lining of a Samsonite coming from Lagos. So you really should never say never.

Anyway, back to Wally and Leroy. Wally had asked his jockey, Pete, to check out Leroy's passport. When Pete did this he spoke to Alpha One and updated him with the situation, including the fact that Montereaux had been inside for knife crime, and was connected to a gang of Mancunian Yardies. Now this was where the Duty Senior Officer in the early years, the Alpha One or, as time progressed, the SIO earned his corn. Here was a connected smuggler almost certainly carrying drugs. Do we run it or do we pull the plug on it now. Do the advantages of the run (possibly more drugs, picking up other people involved, establishing a route, identifying addresses, etc.) outweigh the risks. There is always the risk that you might lose the suspect and the drugs. But on top of that there is the risk to the officers. Alpha One or the SIO, always had at the forefronts of their minds the death of Peter Bennett when he was murdered by Lenny"Teddy Bear" Watkins. Watkins was driving a lorry containing cannabis worth £2.5 million. As Peter Bennett moved in to make the arrest, Watkins shot him dead. He is now doing life.

The risk of violence with Montereaux was particularly relevant. He had a record of violence and he was connected to a violent gang. On the one hand they, the gang, were based in Manchester so would they really have bothered to have come all this way to meet him? But on the other hand Montereaux had no train tickets, although Alpha One was unaware of this at the time, so how was he getting home unless someone was meeting him. Alpha One had to be sure he had enough officers in civvies to overwhelm any possible meeters and greeters. Not just enough to arrest them; that would be two to one; but enough to overwhelm them. Experience had shown that for one thing you never knew how many people there might be meeting them. Secondly it had taught Customs that if those being arrested are overwhelmed they tend to give up without a fight. However if they think they can punch their way out of it because there aren't too many officers, then they will.

**

Alpha One's biggest problem was always the lack of staff. Very often not all the information could be acted upon. It was Alpha One's decision what would be acted on and what wouldn't. Added complications were the different teams own plans and targets. Alpha One would very often have whole teams in their office moaning and putting pressure to be allowed to follow their own plans and drop whatever it was that had been deployed to do. This was particularly true when they were being deployed to work with other Security services. They felt that their plans would be more productive than what Alpha One was asking them to do, and very often they were right. They were experienced and especially the Tarmac teams very productive. Often Alpha One had to be aware of the bigger picture. If MI5 or MI6 were asking for something to be done, maybe a suitcase to be found, which the Tarmac Teams were brilliant at doing, Alpha One would know that it was connected with National Security and was naturally the top priority.

Information from the DLO's was further complicated by the fact that very often they were ex colleagues. So the Alpha Ones perception of the value of the information could be prejudiced, either in a negative or positive way. In the early days a typical bit of info from a DLO might well concern numbers of swallowers on a particular flight. It was not unusual for the DLO in Kingston to pick up information about as many as twenty swallowers on a particular flight. Now Alpha One would have been expecting drug smugglers, both normal mules and swallowers, on this flight. But what this would have warned him or her of, was just how many officers they needed to have in the Green Channel. Sadly very often there would not be enough officers. Alpha One would then have the option of using the Passive Dogs. These beautiful animals could be used around people because as their name suggests, they don't go frantic, they just sit, and maybe indicate by putting a paw on the offending person or piece of baggage. When they did it to the person it was almost as if they were saying, "You're nicked."

Using the Passive Dogs Alpha One would instruct the airline to unload their passengers into the seating area at the Embarkation Gate when they disembark the aircraft. Then simply walk the dog up and down along the lines of passengers. When he or she gets an indication, as stated previously the dog will sit or indicate with a paw. On one notable occasion Alpha One couldn't believe his eyes when the Springer Spaniel actually leant forward, rested his chin on the knee of the suspect, and looked up into his face with those big Spaniel eyes. It was just like his Border Collie when she wanted to go for a walk. Amazing! As if the dog was looking right into his soul

With swallowers of course the dog's effectiveness depended on just how careful the swallower had been when swallowing his packages. The dogs rely on minute particles of dust from the drugs getting on the clothing and on the skin. Sometimes the dog would find nothing but the officers would pick up swallowers in the Green. These people had obviously found a way of swallowing without touching the packages. Probably sitting naked with their clothes well out of the way and then having someone dropping the packages down their throat just like oysters.

**

Samuel was Alpha One and it was manic. He hadn't had time to assess the state of play before the phone started ringing, Senior Officers were sticking their heads round the door looking for information. There was news of a potential swallower over in Terminal 4. Stansted Customs had left a message needing a call back about some anonymous information on the Islamabad later in the day. Harmondsworth, where the prisoners were now housed, had been on, there were urgent Prisoner Reviews to carry out, and one of three swallowers had had the paramedics looking at her but she was now pronounced stable. A decision on whether to move her to Hillingdon Hospital would be taken by the doctor who was on his way. He'd lost a complete team because they'd been stuck on an operation from the previous day and they were now out of hours. There was a little note telling him that the Head of Region was going to pay a "surprise" visit round about 11:00 hours. Then there was a message from the British Airports Authority (BAA) Duty Manager. There had been an incident in the staff canteen involving an officer and BAA wanted blood. When he looked at the teams he had on they weren't brilliant and there was a lot of info to cover.

Sam is feverishly trying to get his head round this lot when the land line rings. The one thing you can never do as Alpha One is ignore the telephone. Any really hot information, anything sensitive, anything where there is a possibility it might be compromised, will come over the land line. So he picks it up. At the same time telling everyone else to keep the noise down.

"Are you the one in control?" A very serious sounding voice rasped down the telephone.

It was a funny way of putting it but Sam was the Control Surveyor, and a bit like the aforementioned Fat Controller from the Tommy the Tank Engine books he was in control.

"Yes I'm the one in control", replied Samuel.

"Activate code Alpha Bravo Tango 00932 Delta immediately" barked the still anonymous voice. And then for good measure:

"Alpha Bravo Tango 00932 Delta immediately, got that?"

Sam repeated the code, took the anonymous persons number and said he would call back in five minutes. He then sat back and wondered just what the bloody hell was going on. Code Alpha Bravo Tango 00932 Delta. Never heard of it. He sat back and thought it through. His anonymous caller had got the wrong control. But he had called a number with the Heathrow dialling code. So what other control could he be looking for? The Police, possibly, but Samuel knew the Police control wasn't based at Heathrow. Special Branch, Immigration, very unlikely. Then a lightning bolt of inspiration hit him. The Control Tower. Of course the Control Tower. The clues in the name.

There's two minutes until 5 minutes is up. He calls them. Yes, yes of course they know what Alpha Bravo Tango 00932 Delta is. It's an emergency helicopter coming in from some Army Base. It's unscheduled and without receiving the code the Control Tower would have assumed some form of attack, and they would have activated another code that involved fighter jets and surface to air missiles. Sam needed a lie down. Just thinking of the near disaster that he had narrowly averted, his legs went all wobbly. Just like Ossie Ardiles at Wembley. He could probably do with a drink. But the lie down and the drink would have to wait because here was the Head of Region sticking his head round the door. The "surprise visit" had started, and right on cue the BAA Station Manager appears looking like a bear with a sore head.

Although not an everyday occurrence Sam's nightmare morning summed up the Alpha One job. You just never knew what would happen next. You never knew what decision you might be needed to make.

For the more soft hearted among you the lady swallower was sent off to Hillingdon and survived. She eventually produced two-hundred and fifty-seven packages containing cocaine and was duly put away in Holloway on full board.

**

As time went on and their reputation grew, they became the focal point for anyone who had anything they wanted to let Customs know about. They knew if they let Alpha One know, then it would be dealt with in the most appropriate way. Or passed on to whoever really needed to know. It wasn't just information for Heathrow, but any information regarding Customs and in particular drugs.

Graham was Alpha One and it was a Sunday evening. It always seemed to happen on a Sunday. The phone rang and it was Barking nick.

"Just thought you might want to know that we've found the body of an elderly Asian female in a skip at the back of Sainsbury's on the Barking Road. No clothes, she's in bin bags. No obvious cause of death so we thought she might have packages inside her that have burst. We're going to open her up so thought you might want to send someone down to retrieve any packages."

Just like that. Why Alpha One, why Heathrow? Stansted was nearer, City Airport was only just down the road. The Custom House by London Bridge was nearer. Our Headquarters in Sea Container House, Blackfriars was nearer. But no, the Police in Barking nick knew that if they informed Alpha One it would get dealt with professionally.

Graham was lucky. It was Sunday and he had plenty of staff. Strange, there were always plenty of staff on a Sunday. He sent a couple of Officers down and sure enough the old lady was full of packages containing heroin. There didn't appear to be any seepage but there obviously was as she had died of a massive overdose. She was of Pakistani origin but there was no way of identifying her. She was almost certainly forced to swallow the drugs.

What a dreadful way for a person to end their life, naked in a skip and full of drugs. Horrible!

**

Neville, or Nev as he was known, was just winding down and he was ready for home, it had been a busy evening watch and Building 820 was full of prisoners of various descriptions. There were still two interviews going on but these would soon be on their way to the Northside Nick for charging. It was all under control. Then the telephone rings:

"Alpha One, this is Barry in the Custody."

The Custody Suite is in Building 820 where the prisoners are held.

"What's up Barry?"

Nev is feverishly trying to work out if he has missed Detention Review. Unlikely because the Custody Officers keep right on top the Reviews. But it's serious if he has because if the Review time has passed the prisoner is being held illegally and is entitled to be released.

"We've got two prisoners here who are looking decidedly iffy. The Paramedics are on their way, but they don't look good."

"Who are they?"

Nev opens his notebook. All the detainees are in there.

"It's the boys from Brazil."

Nev looks at the list and sure enough there are two detainees who are Brazilian on their way in from Rio.

There's not a lot Nev can do, he's no doctor, but he decides to go over to Building 820 where the Custody Suite is housed.

"I'm on my way."

His role will be to support and advise. To make sure the officers are OK and that all proper procedures have been followed. If the worst comes to the worst he will be responsible for informing the police and his own Senior Management. He will also make sure the officers are supported in any way necessary. They will be stressed if not traumatised. They know these people. To Nev they're just names in a notebook but to the four officers who are babysitting they are real people. If they die they will have to cope with that and they will have to be interviewed by the police. Nev will have to make sure that they are looked after. By the time Nev reaches the Custody Suite the paramedics are there. Things have deteriorated. The duty Doctor is also there. It's looking bad for the boys from Brazil.

Thirty minutes later the two men from Brazil are pronounced dead. Probable cause of death a massive overdose. This will be confirmed later at the post mortem. The paramedics remove the bodies. The officers are in shock. The Senior Officer is fussing round like a mother hen making sure his officers are OK. Nev is dealing with the police. They want to carry out interviews straight away. It's now about 1:00 a.m., Nev would rather that they were dealt with in the morning. The officers say they would rather get it over with. Nev returns to his office and starts writing reports. The Senior Officer is arranging counselling for the officers, just in case they need it.

Nev finishes his reports, calls the Custody Suite to make sure he is no longer needed, he's on his mobile if there is. He informs his Senior Manager. It's 3:00 a.m. and he make his way to the car park. He feels incredibly sad. The boys from Brazil were drug smugglers, they knew the risks. But they were desperate pathetic people who did not deserve to die whilst in the process of making someone else very rich.

**

Cash Dogs

The Achilles Heel of the drug smuggling organisation, if there is one, is the need for hard cash. This was especially true in the early years when electronic banking was unheard of. There is no trust among the various parts of the chain that produce, supply, transport, and sell drugs. The old adage "Honour Amongst Thieves" is certainly inappropriate when used in respect of the illegal drugs industry. There is also the fact that cash transactions leave no audit trail. Credit Cards, Cheques, Bankers Drafts, Promissory Notes, electronic transfers etc., all leave a potential audit trail. Break into the trail at one point and who knows where it might lead. Although over the years the cartels have become more and more sophisticated, and offshore Bank Accounts have become harder and harder to unravel and identify, the need for hard cash is still there. So this leaves the organisation with a problem. The drugs are brought over to the UK and sold for British pounds. Those pounds are laundered into dollars or Euros. But a certain percentage of that laundered money has to be physically moved out of the country back to where the drugs are bought, in order to start the ball rolling again. Some of this can be facilitated by buying expensive items such as high performance motor cars; shipping them back and selling them for cash. But this takes time, and just as with any other business, time means money. On top of that, just like any other business there are always cash flow problems. One of the reasons that one of largest cartels; the Columbian Cali Cartel; eventually ceased trading, was a lack of available cash. The cash flow dried up, bribes couldn't be paid, so arrests were made. New supplies couldn't be purchased so people left, joined other cartels, or informed to the police or the US DEA. This all means that money has to be physically moved from A to B to keep the business solvent.

So this is where the Cash Dogs come in useful. These are dogs that can actually smell cash in suitcases. They're worth their weight in gold. They were, and are, mainly used on suitcases leaving the country.

As the outward bound passengers on high risk flights check in, the suitcases disappear through the flaps behind the check-in operator. They then all pass through an x-ray machine that is looking for bombs and explosives. As they pass through to the other side of the x-ray machine the dogs do a sort of balancing act on top of the suitcases and sniff out the cash inside. It's an amazing sight to see as the suitcases go through at quite a speed. The dogs will detect quite small sums of money. On a person this can be as little as a five pound note. A combination of the ink and the fine spray of plastic, which is applied to make the notes more resilient, is what the dogs can smell.

**

If Customs ever needed reminding how important the moving of hard cash was, it came in a remarkable incident in 1976. Two Officers were sat in the Tarmac Office. They were a team that had what might appear to be a strange role for Customs. They were a team that had a special responsibility for checking out Temporary Importation (TI) cars. That is cars which had been imported on a temporary basis but they had overstayed the TI limits. Steve and Bert were sitting in the Tarmac Office having a sandwich. As told to the author, Steve had cheese and tomato, and Bert had ham and mustard. They'd been busy. They'd been on since 07.00. They had had a lot of paper work to do, and it was near the end of the month so they'd had overtime sheets to do and travel expenses to sort out. All important stuff, but it meant they'd been stuck in the office most of the morning. So they were ready for something to do. The Duty Senior Officer (DSO) poked his head round the corner and told them that the Control Tower had just informed him that there was Cessna, registration G-AL something something, had just asked for clearance to proceed to Deauville. It had apparently landed from Blackbushe Airport about two hours ago. It was a strange flight pattern. Why would a light aircraft fly into Heathrow from Blackbushe, only 30 miles down the road, incur the horrendous landing fees at Heathrow, and then take off again to go to Deauville just across the Channel. It has to be said that nobody was really thinking drugs. Not going out, not exportation. Even though at the time the UK was the world leader in the production of LSD. Isn't it nice to know we led the world in something even if it had to be LSD production? This was before that fateful day on the 26th of March 1977 when Operation Julie swooped on eighty-seven homes and premises and effectively put an end to it for a while.

The DSO told the Control Tower that Customs would like to talk to the pilot, so the aircraft was sent back to the General Aviation Terminal (GAT) on the far side of the airport. This was where the light aircraft were parked. In those days this area was very easy to access, the planes were parked literally a stone's throw from a public road.

Steve and Bert decided to get their skates on. This was unusual for this pair, they weren't renowned for their haste. However they wanted to be there when the plane got back to the GAT, and they had to go through the tunnel that went below the runway, as the GAT was on the South side right next to where Terminal Four would be in 1986. They were in a hurry just in case it had called into Heathrow to pick something up, and whoever had delivered it was still there, and would take it off again before they got there. If they did, they could be out of the gate and on their way in a couple of minutes. But they still weren't really thinking drugs.

Luckily there must have been a lot of runway traffic because just as they turned the corner Cessna G-AL something something was arriving on stand. How nice was that, just on time. No sign of any cars hanging around, although later enquiries would show that there had been three cars there about half an hour before it took off.

As soon as the engines had died Bert approached the aircraft and opened the door. Now the Cessna, probably a type 150L, was only about 24 feet in length, and the cockpit was probably about a third of its total length. So the boys were quite happy that having reached the stand if there was something to hide they would be able to find it. Nothing could have prepared Bert for what he was about to see. He opened the door and looked to his left at the pilot and the pilot was looking over his shoulder back at Bert. The first thing that Bert noticed was that the pilot (who for legal reasons we cannot name and who we will call Mr Moneybags) had a thermos flask and a Tupperware box with his cheese and ham sandwiches in. Both were tucked down by his side. The second thing he saw was "money". Bundles and bundles of cash everywhere. And it was obviously money. It was all tied up with elastic bands it wasn't in brown paper parcels or plastic bags so you couldn't see what was inside. All Bert could see was bundle after bundle of five, ten, and twenty pound notes. There was almost no room for the pilot to get out. There was approximately £2.8 million pounds in used notes. Bert and Steve found out later that the maximum take-off weight for a Cessna is about 200 kilos more than the aircraft weight. This must have been close to the limit.

When Bert told the story he said that it was a bizarre situation which was made all the more bizarre by the fact that he couldn't get his first though out of his head. As he put it, he saw all this money and all he could think was:-

"You've got all this money, and yet you've still brought sandwiches and coffee. Surely you could have afforded a decent meal in Deauville." It was the same as getting an irreverent thought in church, it just wouldn't go away.

The pilot of course didn't have a clue who all this money belonged to. He didn't know where it had come from. He had been paid a thousand pounds in cash. This was in a separate envelope. He had the name of the man who was supposed to be meeting him in Deauville. This of course turned out to be false. He had the names of the men who had approached him in The Ely, a pub near Camberley on the A30, about a mile from Blackbushe Airport. But they were obviously false. His whole demeanour was of innocent amazement. "Do you think it's a bit iffy?" He asked Bert and Steve. The Control Point by the GAT had the Registration numbers of the cars that had been seen by the aircraft side, but they were hire cars. And surprise surprise the names they had been hired under were false. It was amazing to think that £2.8 million had been transferred from these cars into the plane in broad daylight and less than fifty yards from a Control Point manned by Security Guards. We always had our theories about how ineffective security was in those days and this certainly confirmed it. The aircraft belonged to the pilot, Mr Moneybags, who lived in Esher, and who, on the face of it had no criminal connections. The Police were involved but they couldn't get any further. There had been no big Bank, or Gold Bullion jobs in the recent past. Fingerprints revealed lots of prints but no matches.

The money was seized and the pilot said it wasn't his so he couldn't appeal. But the difficult thing was, what was he actually doing wrong? This was twenty-five years before the Proceeds of Crime Act 2002 would put the onus on the criminal to prove that their cash or property hadn't come from crime, and it was ten years before the Drug Trafficking Offences Act 1986 would allow Customs to strip criminals of their illegally obtained gains. The only piece of legislation the HM Customs were left with was Section 22 of the Exchange Control Act of 1947. This Act however did not provide penalties, only sanctions. The obvious sanction in this instance was to seize the money. This was done and the Exchequer was £2.8 million richer. But nobody was ever prosecuted.

There were lots of unanswered questions. Mr Moneybags looked at thousands of "mugshots". He either couldn't or wouldn't identify his benefactors. It was obviously hot money. But why was it hot? The vast amounts of money involved in the drug trade were still largely a mystery. Later, seven-hundred and fifty thousand pounds would be recovered from Operation Julie (mentioned above), and it would be years before Howard Marks, that is Mr Nice, went into print to let us know the huge sums that could be made from cannabis smuggling. But this was one of the first signs Customs had of the vast sums that were swilling around in the coffers of the drug barons.

**

It was a Saturday morning about 11.00 am, and Alpha One, Jim, was busy. He was short of staff and he had information coming out of his ears. The one good thing was he had some local CIU and some of the Investigators from up town hanging around. They'd been involved in an operation that hadn't materialised into anything. So should anything worthwhile turn up he knew they could manage it. All the usual stuff was going on. There was a 24 hour PACE review to do in Building 820 where Customs had their cells. After prisoners have been held for 24 hours their detention must be reviewed by someone of the rank of Police Superintendent or Customs Surveyor, to make sure there is good cause for them to continue to be held without charge. This was a serious matter and the prisoner would have his or her Solicitor present. There were two Officers wanting EMITs. Then over the radio Jim could hear that there was a dog loose on the Tarmac and one of his Tarmac Teams was involved in trying to apprehend it. He did put out a general call to any Dog Team in the area to see if they could help, but the sarcasm was lost on the officers. There was some discussion about borrowing a couple of Kevlar vests from the Firearms Team just in case they actually found this particularly vicious animal.

As he was coming to grips with a whole load of information from the DLO in Kingston, and trying to assess just which high-risk flights could be covered and by which teams, the land line rang. It was the DITs. It was a close friend of Jim's by the name of Martyn. The information was good. A Bolivian gentleman by the name of Cortez (which is a bit like Smith or Jones in Bolivia) was arriving on the Miami. Nothing too amazing in that particular piece of information. There would be a lot of Bolivians on the Miami, and a fair chance one or two might be called Cortez. But the interesting thing was that a man by the name of Cortez, with the same Christian names had left the UK about five months previously carrying a large sum of money, in cash, in his suitcase. The Cash Dog, a Springer, had been operating on the bags destined for the out bound Miami. It had given a strong indication that there was cash inside a large soft sided "Tourister" suitcase. In fact the dog was going berserk. The dog handler using the enormous bunch of keys that most Officers who operated on the Tarmac seemed to have, opened the suitcase. Inside there were bundles of Euros to the approximate value of fifteen-thousand pounds. The CIU were called in and the Baggage Tag led to a person by the name Juan Angelo Cortez. The decision was taken to let the money run, and to leave Cortez in blissful ignorance. Why let the money run? It was obviously drug money that had been laundered from British Pounds into Euros. But by now Customs weren't happy with just snipping off the limbs. They wanted the people behind the drugs. So Cortez was obviously important and trusted by whichever organisation he was connected to. He wasn't just a mule. The organisation wouldn't have trusted a mule with that much money. The average payment to a swallower at that time was five-hundred pounds. If someone is desperate enough to risk their life for five-hundred pounds it's probably not a good idea to trust them with fifteen-thousand pounds. So the decision was taken to let him go and wait for him to put his head above the parapet at some later date. DLO's were informed, not just ours but all those from other countries with whom we had agreements to share information. And, as it turned out, most importantly, so were the DITs.

So this was the information Jim received. Juan Angelo Cortez was arriving on the American Airways flight from Miami which was landing in about half an hour. If this was the same Cortez this could be a big one. The Investigation teams, two local and one from up town were immediately alerted and were very interested. Immigration were alerted as it was vital Cortez was identified before he reached the Green Channel. Jim didn't want him turned out. There would be a lot of activity in the Green because of other information that had come in from the DLO in Bogota. So as there would be a lot going on Jim arranged for what he called a "light tug" to take place. That is once Cortez was identified at Immigration he would be observed in the Reclaim Hall and then when he went through the Green Channel an Officer would stop him and have a brief word with him. This was to allay any suspicions he might have if he saw lots of people off of the Miami being stopped but he wasn't. Almost a double bluff.

A really experienced Officer called John carried out the "light tug". Cortez had a good story. He had a hotel reservation, credit cards, times and places of business meetings he was going to attend. All fictitious of course. But it was a good story just as you would expect from someone who was part of the organisation. He was allowed to proceed and he was then being followed by several of the uptown Investigators and the local CIU. He made his way to Starbucks, bought himself a coffee and sat down in the far corner watching the entrance. Cortez had been there for about forty-five minutes when a man with two hard sided suitcases approached him and appeared to ask him if the seat next to him was free. This man was Columbian and had arrived on the Bogota flight. He was carrying nearly twenty kilos of cocaine concealed in double tops and bottoms of the suitcases. He bought himself a coffee and sat next to Cortez. Cortez bought himself a second cup, you would have thought coming from South America he would have had better taste. They then sat there for about thirty minutes watching the entrance. Starbucks was in a perfect position for them. It was placed just inside the Terminal right next to the car park lifts and by the exit to the taxis. It was ideal because there was no reason for anyone to hang around for any length of time. So anybody watching them would stand out like a sore thumb. However by this stage in their development our Investigators were very professional and there are a variety of ways of watching someone or something without it being 'bleedin' obvious.

Eventually they both got up. They gave up any pretence of not being together and proceeded to the taxi rank. There they took a taxi to the Renaissance Hotel on the A4. The taxi driver must have been very new or he was about to go home because they didn't normally take such short fares. Or perhaps he just ripped them off so he didn't care how short the journey was. Anyway they were deposited in the Renaissance Hotel, right next door to the Custom House. Cortez booked them in to a double room and off they went. Our boys and girls promptly introduced themselves to the Hotel Management and took over every available room around the one occupied by Cortez and the Colombian courier. Now all they had to do was wait. For once they didn't have to wait too long. After about an hour and a half, two dusky looking gentlemen in jeans and casual jackets, arrived carrying two very empty looking holdalls. Later it turned out they were also Bolivian, had arrived the previous day and were also staying in the Renaissance. How nice and cosy was that? There was another delay, but only about an hour this time. Then the two Bolivians left still carrying the holdalls but the holdalls now looked an awful lot heavier. This was all very quick in fact it was unusually quick. Cortez must have been very sure that he hadn't been followed, or of course it could have been that he'd done it so many times he was getting a bit too confident. But it hadn't seemed like that when he was sitting in Starbucks.

They took a cab to Osterley Tube Station and went into the Underground Station. When it became obvious they were heading for the Tube the Investigators consulted with their SIO and Alpha One about whether or not to pull the plug and arrest the men. It was unusual in this type of scenario for the SIO to consult with Alpha One. But following people on the Underground was dangerous. Nobody was happy following suspects into the Underground and normally it wouldn't happen. But it was so obvious what was about to take place it was too good an opportunity to miss. Plus the Underground on a Saturday would be pretty quiet, especially at a station like Osterley. Some of the volatility would be diminished. So down they went. Eight men and women on foot. Six above ground in unmarked cars. The cars just headed gently towards the next station on the map and waited to hear from their colleagues, then the next station, then the next, and so on. With officers getting on and off at each station. Our two Bolivians took the Piccadilly Line as far as Earls Court. Here they crossed over to the District Line. The watchers got a message to the cars telling them they were on the District Line heading north. When the Bolivians reached Notting Hill Gate station they got off and left the station. They then walked very slowly and casually down Notting Hill Gate towards Holland Park. The teams in the cars were coming around Shepherds Bush and were getting there as fast as they could. About two hundred yards down Notting Hill Gate is a pub called the Uxbridge Arms. They turned left just before the pub and came into Uxbridge Street. Directly opposite was a small coffee shop called the Cafe Med. Our operatives were already in both places. The Bolivians stood outside having a cigarette and obviously waiting and watching. It was now difficult for the followers as it was quiet in the back streets. Two followers walked past them and went straight down Callcott Street. One of the cars drove down Uxbridge Street. They were still there. A woman Officer walked round from Farm Place towards the two men. As she got close to them they finally put out their cigarettes, threw them on the floor, and went into the cafe. She quickly let her SO, an ex-Heathrow Officer called Pete, know and followed them into the cafe. She spotted her two colleagues at the back of the café. Luckily it was busy. The TV was on and the football results were coming through. The female Officer, we'll call her Caroline, couldn't believe what she was seeing. The two Bolivians were quite openly sitting and chatting with two white males. These two, while pretending to watch the football results, had their eyes everywhere. They'd been there a quite a time, the two Officers had seen them come in and sit at a table for four. They'd placed themselves diagonally across the table and they had spread out so nobody could sit in the other two seats. Caroline bought herself a tea and sat at the only table that was completely unoccupied. Unfortunately it was directly behind the four men. So although she could see them and also catch snatches of their conversation, she couldn't let Pete know what was going on. Not even using her lapel mike. One of the holdalls was poking out from under the table and presumably the other was under the table. It seemed unbelievable that the switch was going to take place in a busy cafe in the middle of the day. But maybe these villains knew each other too well.

After about ten minutes a second Officer, a young Irishman called Joe, went into the cafe. Made no secret of the fact that he was there and asked the man serving, "How did the Gunners get on?" Joe, never heard the answer. He got the shock of his life when he casually turned round to take a look at the two white faces. He not only knew them, he'd been involved when one of their houses was busted about eighteen months before. These men, Greenaway and Tarrant were the two top men in their own medium sized operation that operated in the East End. Joe got himself into a position where he could use his lapel mike and appraised Pete of the situation. Pete contacted Alpha One, his own Surveyor, the SIO, being for whatever reason unreachable, and it was decided to pull the plug on the op. They didn't dare wait. If the four men had left the café and split up they didn't have enough officers to follow all four of them.

It was too dangerous to make the arrests in the cafe so they did have to wait a short time. Jim was relieved when the SIO came back on air and endorsed the decision to arrest the men as soon as they left the café. Eventually the two Bolivians left. They were followed as far as Notting Hill Gate Station. Then, well out of sight of the café as they entered Notting Hill station, they were arrested, cuffed, and put in separate cars. The rest of the team carried on waiting. One of the men, Greenaway, got up and left the cafe. No need to follow him too far, his car was parked just about 20 yards from the cafe door. Two minutes later Tarrant appeared carrying the two holdalls, as he reached the car Greenaway sprung the boot, and as Tarrant was about to deposit the holdalls in the boot Pete and his team pounced.

What a result. Twenty kilos of Coke, one courier, one middleman, two Bolivian hierarchy, all from a cartel called the Cali cartel, which has now been declared bankrupt. In addition two East End villains with their own operation. There were some who thought that there probably was a third man, the money man, connected to Tarrant and Greenaway. And that was why Cortez was here. The operation was so slick it had obviously been going for some time, so maybe he was here to re-negotiate the contract. Or maybe he was here because they didn't trust the Columbian mule. Or maybe Tarrant and Greenaway were expecting to meet with him, which is why they were involved in something they would normally leave to their minions. Whatever the reason it was the most successful operation JIm was ever involved in. And it all came about because of a Springer Spaniel with a very delicate nose. The cash dogs really were worth their weight in gold.

**

In conclusion, an amazing fact about the dogs that can smell cash in suitcases is their sex. The other dogs used by Customs/Border Force, that is the two types of drug dogs, the tobacco dogs, the explosives dogs, the dogs that smell radio-active material, even the dogs that sniff out products of animal origin. All of these can be either dogs or bitches. But the ones that can smell cash in suitcases, these dogs are all bitches!!! I just wonder what David Attenborough would have to say about that!

**

Airbridge and After

The pursuit of the two legged drug mule as it is described in this book, carries on, but as it has continued several factors have come into play to make it a more even contest. The DLO system has continued to improve and to become more effective. The formation of SOCA followed by the National Crime Agency has removed many of the barriers that existed between the Police and Customs, and this linked with DLO's has created a system of upstream disruption that is having a real impact on the supply reaching the UK. As stated previously the National Agency for Substance Misuse and the charity Drugscope (before its sad demise) certainly support this claim.

Sadly some things have not helped, the merger of the Detection Branch of HMRC- previously part of HM Customs and Excise- with HM Immigration to form the Border Force within the Border Agency, has been a retrograde step. It should, and still could be a positive move. The workings of Customs Detection Officers and HM Immigration Officers do dovetail in a way that should produce a more effective organisation at the frontier. However the lack of flexibility and mobility displayed by ex HM Immigration Officers means that when queues at Passport Control become unacceptable the fully mobile Customs Officers are moved from the Green Channels to assist with the queue busting. This is not the fault of the individual Immigration Officers more the fault of their previous managers who allowed restrictive practices within HM Immigration to become established.

**

In 2001/2 the number of swallowers apprehended reached epidemic level with seven-hundred and thirty being caught at Heathrow and Gatwick. The Collector at that time decided it could not continue. Those seven-hundred and thirty swallowers stayed for an average of three and a half days they were watched for every minute of their stay by two officers. This meant six officers for every 24 hours, a total of twenty-one staff days for every prisoner. Multiplied by seven-hundred and thirty prisoners it meant that the swallower problem was taking up over fifteen-thousand staff days. On average after days off, Public Holidays and annual leave had been taken away, the average officer worked two-hundred and twenty days a year, assuming he or she wasn't sick at all that year. This meant seventy staff years were being used up purely and simply on looking after swallowers. And the swallowers were only carrying on average half a kilo of Class A drugs. A relatively small amount of drugs. On occasion Alpha One's whole shift would be taken up dealing with requests for EMITs, dealing with requests for x-rays, and reviewing the detention of prisoners arrested previously. This situation was exacerbated for the Alpha Ones when a brand new prisoner holding facility was built off airport. This meant that instead of walking a couple of hundred yards to carry out their reviews of detention, they had a fifteen minute drive both ways.

As far as the management were concerned, this was unacceptable. Swallowers were only bringing in half a kilo of coke or smack at time. A double sided suitcase would bring in ten kilos and be dealt with within twelve hours by two officers. So the seven-hundred and thirty swallowers brought in at the most 365 kilos, 36 couriers carrying ten kilos each would bring in the same amount but only use just over three staff years.

There had to be a solution. They couldn't reduce the observation regime, the prisoners had to be watched. Swallowers are at risk and they are desperate so they are prepared to do things that normal people wouldn't even consider doing. Things like passing packages and re-swallowing them. So two officers had to watch each prisoner. It was non-negotiable. The Collector, decided the situation could not be allowed to be continue.

 Most of the swallowers were coming from Jamaica so eyes were turned to Kingston, and the Collector negotiated with the authorities there. The negotiations appeared to last forever. It was so politically sensitive it couldn't be rushed. Eventually the legal complications of foreign (UK) Customs Officers working in Jamaica were overcome and officers from the UK were posted to Kingston. Operation Airbridge was up and running. This was obviously a particularly sensitive role. At this point something happened that at the time didn't come across as particularly important, but in fact was vital to the success of the operation. A Senior Officer, we'll call him Chris, a Spurs supporter and an ex Public School boy, was given the job of kicking it all off. Whoever made this decision should get a gong. Chris along with his sidekick Guy were just the right men to handle this politically sensitive job. In no time at all Airbridge was reducing the number of swallowers. The following year only one-hundred and eighty were apprehended at Heathrow. On top of that they were giving information about passengers who they thought were suspicious, but who had come up negative on the Ionscan machine that they were using to detect suspected swallowers.

Another benefit that accrued from Chris's appointment came about because of his natural skill as a diplomat. Although some people referred to this skill as "bullshit", it did have the required affect. Not only were no feathers ruffled, the team were valued and appreciated by their Jamaican hosts. Chris's team actually launched a charity to help orphaned Jamaican children.

Because it was so successful Airbridge was eventually followed by Operation Westbridge in Accra, Ghana. Accra, wasn't as high up the list as Lagos or Bogota, but they were both considered too dangerous to place UK officers there. It might not be perfect but let's face it one-hundred and eighty swallowers a year is a lot more acceptable than seven-hundred and thirty.

The numbers continue to fall at Heathrow. At the time of going to press in 2016 the annual number is approximately seventy. This further reduction is mainly due to the moving of direct Caribbean flights from Heathrow to Gatwick. And at Gatwick? Surprise, surprise the numbers have risen to around one-hundred and fifty. Things move on. The EMIT machine, which was at one time the main tool in the battle, is now mainly redundant. The swallowers now use masking agents to give false negatives when their urine is tested. The officers now use soft x-ray Compass equipment to take x-rays themselves. Technology plays an increasing role in the battle against the drug cartels, but it all starts with an officer liking the look of someone coming through the Green. Or wondering why a particular suitcase isn't as flexible as it should be. Or maybe a dog likes the smell of a bag on the Reclaim Belt.

**

The Pursuit of the Two Legged Drug Mule continues. There will never be an outright winner in this race. The dedication, hard work, and ability to learn, displayed by the officers at Heathrow and Gatwick helped to keep the finger in the dam. It helped stem the tide until agencies such as SOCA and the National Crime Agency could get involved. However all of that will be overturned if queues at the Passport Controls in Heathrow are allowed to dissipate the numbers of officers operating in the Green Channels, the Red Channels, behind the Terminals on the Tarmac Areas, and in the Freight Sheds.

The End

Glossary

Airbridge	An initiative to catch swallowers before they leave their homeland. By basing UK Officers in Jamaica.
APO/AO	Assistant Preventive Officer, later Assistant Officer.
BAA	British Airports Authority.
Babysitting	Jargon which refers to the minding of prisoners who have swallowed drugs.
Baggage Tag	The label affixed to a suitcase by the airline staff at check-in. The matching tag is stuck on the ticket.
Box	Interview room.
Bucket shop	A shop that sells cheap airline tickets.
C1422	A written declaration completed by the passenger when a suitcase is missing.
Candy/Candy cane.	Cocaine.
Cannabrum	A mixture of white over proof rum and herbs containing some cannabis.
Carousel	Baggage belt in the Reclaim Hall.

Case Officer	The Officer who has responsibility for interviewing the offender and preparing the offence for Court. This is usually the Officer who makes the original detection.
Class A	Refers to the drugs designated most dangerous in the Misuse of Drugs Act. Normally refers to either Cocaine or Heroin, and occasionally to Crack Cocaine or liquid Cannabis.
Coke	Cocaine.
Concourse	The area after passengers have left the Customs area where people congregate to meet arriving passengers.
CIU	Customs Intelligence Unit. Plain clothes officers used for further investigation after initial interceptions have been made.
Control Point	A place within the terminals where BAA Security check for firearms etc.
Custody/Custodised	A person is taken into Custody after being arrested. They are then dealt with under the Police and Criminal Evidence Act. The Custody Officer makes sure the prisoners rights are adhered to. They are Custodised.
Customs Codes	The books of instructions under which Customs Officer operated.

Cut	Slang for mixed. Drugs are mixed with other substances before they are sold.
DEA	The US Drugs Enforcement Agency.
Dirty Bag/Suitcase	Slang for the bag or suitcase containing drugs.
DITs	Detection Information teams. Their role was to check passenger lists against lists of suspects.
DLO	Drugs Liaison Officer. An Officer based abroad to gather information about potential drug importations into the UK.
Dump	Jargon for a bowel motion
DSO	This was an Officer who in the early days would be responsible for day to day deployment. Not to be confused with Alpha One.
Echolac	A make of suitcase. Normally hard sided.
Elvive	A proprietary shampoo brand.
EMIT	Enzyme Multiplied Immunoassay Test. A Urine test for drugs.
Ex-pat	An ex patriot. Someone who has emigrated from the UK, to work and live abroad.
Eyeball	Jargon meaning the target can be seen.

Field test	A test carried out on substances suspected of being drugs in order to get an initial indication of what it might be.
Firearms Team	A team based on the Tarmac for control of firearms arriving and departing on aircraft.
Fix	A fix; a dose of drugs; a shot of drugs.
GAT	General Aviation Terminal. A small Terminal alongside Terminal 4, used by private aircraft.
Gear	Slang for Cannabis.
Hashish/hash	A form of cannabis resin most widely associated with Asia.
Herb	Slang for cannabis.
IB/ID	Investigation Branch or Division.
IC1	Ethnicity code for Caucasian Northern European.
IC3	Ethnicity code for Afro- Caribbean.
Interview Room	The room where offence interviews are carried out. Also referred to as "the box."
KLM	Dutch National Airline.
Jockey	Witness during an interview.

Joint	Slang for a cigarette made of cannabis.
Kevlar Vest	Bullet proof vest.
Light Aircraft	A generic term for a non-scheduled flight. Normally a small aircraft carrying very few passengers and no cargo.
Light Tug	Intercepting a suspect but not looking in their bags. Just confirming their identity.
LHR	London Heathrow Airport.
Lock knife	A knife where it is possible to lock the blade in the open position. It is illegal to possess, but strangely, not to sell these knives.
LOMO	London Overseas Mail Office.
Minder	A person accompanying a mule especially used with swallowers.
Mo Bay	Montego Bay in Jamaica.
Mule	A person of low value employed to import drugs. A courier.
Nick	Police cells/Prison.
Officer	An Officer of HM Customs/Border Force.
officer	When a small o is used this indicates a generic term for either an Officer or an Assistant Officer.

OITs	Operational Intelligence Teams.
Opiate	A generic term for drugs produced from the poppy.
PACE	The Police and Criminal Evidence Act 1984. The Act that laid down rules about how prisoners should be treated.
Paki Black	A particularly strong type of cannabis resin high in tetrahydrocannabinol (THC) the constituent that has the pleasure effect in cannabis.
PK/ Pakair	Pakistan International Airways flight.
Pot	Slang for cannabis.
Profile	The general parameters used to identify a potential drug smuggler. A pen portrait.
Punter	Slang for passenger or offender.
Reclaim Hall	The area where passengers collect their baggage after it has been unloaded from the aircraft.
Red Eye flights	A reference to flights from the Eastern seaboard of the USA. So called because you lost a nights sleep because of the time change.

Rip off bags	Suitcases or bags removed by criminal gangs- who are also airport workers- before they reach the Reclaim Hall. They are then taken out of a gate where there is no Customs presence.
Rip on bags.	Bags put on an aircraft without being checked in.
Search Box	A small room, normally adjacent to the Green Channel where search of persons could take place.
Seizure	A seizure is the finding and confiscating of goods. In most instances it refers to drugs.
Switch bag routine	Method of smuggling using two identical bags.
SIO	Senior Investigation Officer.
Smack	Heroin.
Snort	Cocaine.
Snow	Cocaine.
SOP	A search of a suspects person.
Stand	Parking place for aircraft on the Tarmac.
Swallower	A person with an internal concealment.
Tannoy	Loudspeaker system.

Tarmac teams.	Small teams of officers who worked in the Tarmac Areas.
THC	Tetrahydrocannabinol. The psychoactive constituent of cannabis.
The Tarmac	Generic term for the area used by aircraft.
TI	Temporary Importation.
Twist	A way of packaging small quantities of drugs. The drugs are placed in a type of cling wrap and this is twisted and covered with sticky tape.
Upstream disruption.	Disrupting the flow of drugs at the source.
VAT Refund Desk	The point at which outward passengers produce the goods on which they are claiming a refund of VAT paid.
Woodstock	A music festival held annually at Bethel near New York.
Yardies	The Yardies are members of gangs that originated in Kingston Jamaica. The term originated from the gangs that grew up in Government built estates in Trenchtown, a suburb of Kingston. Each estate was built around a courtyard and this was where the gangs congregated. The word courtyard was shortened to yard and the gang members became "Yardies."